A CITIZEN'S GUIDE TO

IMPEACHMENT

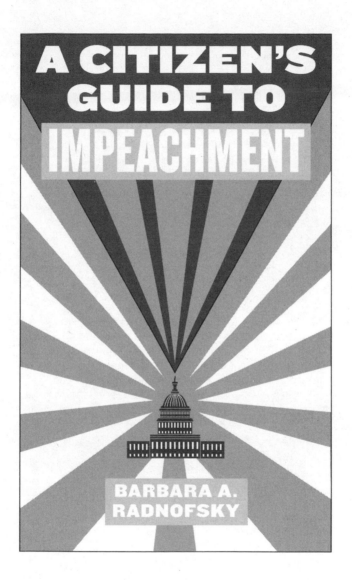

A CITIZEN'S GUIDE TO
IMPEACHMENT

BARBARA A. RADNOFSKY

MELVILLE HOUSE
BROOKLYN · LONDON

A CITIZEN'S GUIDE TO IMPEACHMENT

Copyright © 2017 by Barbara A. Radnofsky

First published by Melville House Publishing, September 2017

Melville House Publishing		8 Blackstock Mews
46 John Street	and	Islington
Brooklyn, NY 11201		London N4 2BT

mhpbooks.com

facebook.com/mhpbooks

@melvillehouse

ISBN: 978-1-61219-705-0

Library of Congress Cataloging-in-Publication Data

Names: Radnofsky, Barbara Ann, 1956- author.
Title: A citizen's guide to impeachment / Barbara A. Radnofsky.
Description: Brooklyn : Melville House, 2017. | Includes bibliographical references and index.
Identifiers: LCCN 2017035521 (print) | LCCN 2017036541 (ebook) | ISBN 9781612197067 (reflowable) | ISBN 9781612197050 (paperback)
Subjects: LCSH: Impeachments--United States. | BISAC: POLITICAL SCIENCE / Political Process / General. | LAW / Government / Federal. | POLITICAL SCIENCE / Constitutions.
Classification: LCC KF4958 (ebook) | LCC KF4958 .R33 2017 (print) | DDC 342.73/062--dc23
LC record available at https://lccn.loc.gov/2017035521

Designed by Fritz Metsch

Printed in the United States of America

1 3 5 7 9 10 8 6 4 2

CONTENTS

Introduction 3

1. Origins of Impeachment Law 6

2. Legal Principles and Processes of Impeachment . . . 18

3. Federal Impeachments in the United States 31

Conclusion 85

Notes 89

Bibliography 147

A CITIZEN'S GUIDE TO

IMPEACHMENT

INTRODUCTION

In the United States, impeachment is a constitutional process by which Congress can remove high officials, including the president, the vice president, federal judges, and cabinet members, from office.

The Americans who fought in the Revolutionary War had a clear sense of the dangers of—and how to combat—a tyrannical, badly functioning, negligent, or incapacitated official in power. They foresaw U.S. civil officers as human beings prone to the same harmful tendencies and disabilities as the British king and his minions.

The remarkably well-educated American victors thoughtfully adapted British law[1] to suit the needs of the new United States. They'd debated, reworked, and polished language to forge a constitution containing what we know as the "Impeachment Clause." The new American statesmen wanted a noncriminal, orderly process—not "tumults and insurrections"[2]—to deal with the "misconduct of public men," as they focused on injuries done to "society itself."[3] Related constitutional clauses that describe the process give Congress (the legislative branch of government) sole power to impeach and remove a badly performing high official.

The U.S. impeachment process can result in the removal—but not the criminal punishment—of a U.S. public official who would cause substantial harm:[4] "The President, Vice President and all civil Officers of the United States, shall be removed from Office on Impeachment for, and Conviction of, Treason,[4] Bribery, or other high Crimes and Misdemeanors." U.S. Const. Art. II, Sec. 4.

The special phrase "high Crimes and Misdemeanors" is lifted directly from ancient British impeachment law and forms the cornerstone of the U.S. impeachment process. It is a term (legally, a "term of art") that bears no resemblance to what we know as "crimes" or "misdemeanors" today. It requires no charging of a crime, no intent to do a wrong,[6] and no law-breaking. When presenting a case for impeachment, Congress may charge (and has charged) civil officers as acting with intent, treachery, criminal misconduct, and law-breaking, but the Constitution requires no proof of such—none—in order to impeach.

The United States Congress has impeached and convicted officials regardless of their mental state—even a person conceded as "insane," in the words of the nineteenth century, as well as persons capable under the law of forming intent. Congress has also impeached calculating, treasonous,[7] corrupt, swindling, or profiteering officials who could substantially harm us.

While many of these stories involve crooks and swindlers who intentionally betrayed trust, sexually assaulted their employees, bribed, stole, sold out their country to enhance the value of their vast landholdings, violated America's foreign policies, fomented war, covered up misdeeds, obstructed justice, committed perjury, and tampered with witnesses, the key factor in considering the impeachability of public officials for "other high Crimes and Misdemeanors" is the harm they can cause;[8] it's not the motive or intent of the official. The greater the potential for harm, the greater the case for impeachment and removal.[9]

This book traces American impeachment history from the country's founding to today, using the nineteen cases of U.S.

impeachment of judges, a cabinet member, a senator, and presidents, plus other important examples of impeachment activity that did not reach the stage of formal House impeachment. But behind the history of the Impeachment Clause in the United States lie centuries of British law and legal practice related to impeachment, which greatly influenced the Founding Fathers' thinking as they created our system of government laid out in the Constitution. Our foundational documents, including the Constitution and its phrase "high Crimes and Misdemeanors," are interpreted by looking to the thinking—that is, the intent—of the Founding Fathers and framers of our country's foundational documents.[10]

So, while it's important to understand that harm to society is the significant element emerging in the history of U.S. impeachment cases, it's equally important to know what the Founding Fathers' intentions were as they debated, crafted, and finalized the Constitution's impeachment clause. The Constitution was written and adopted at a national convention in Philadelphia in 1787 and then became effective in 1788 as a result of votes in state ratifying conventions. The Founding Fathers recorded for posterity their intent to adapt the British law of impeachment, as they displayed—in articles, books, argument, and advocacy at Constitutional Convention debates and then on the floor of Congress—a sophisticated understanding of British history, law, and terminology adapted for use in American impeachment proceedings.

1

ORIGINS OF IMPEACHMENT LAW

In the twentieth century, scholars argued about whether they, or the public, needed any knowledge of British law in the context of impeachment. One school of thought has suggested that the writers of the Constitution, and the Constitution-ratifying convention delegates, lacked specialized knowledge of British law and, therefore, modern students of impeachment need no such knowledge either.[11] These demonstrably incorrect assumptions, if believed, would rob us of understanding the intent and purpose of the Founding Fathers for use of the Impeachment Clause.

January 4, 2018, marks the 250th anniversary of the 1768 publication in the *Boston Gazette* of Josiah Quincy, Jr.'s, article calling attention to English impeachments "for high treason in subverting the fundamental laws and introducing arbitrary power." The article ended with "a ringing call to follow these examples" of impeachment actions.[12]

Within two decades of the *Boston Gazette*'s publication, the United States of America had declared independence, fought and won a war against England, tried to exist under a "Confederation" of States, and then adopted a federal system to replace the states' confederation. The new Constitution, revised and polished in Philadelphia at the Constitutional Convention, emerged with our current "Impeachment Clause."

In deciding on language and voting for the Impeachment Clause, the Founding Fathers relied on their experiences and expertise in English law and its application in America. Many Founding Fathers studied law in England as well as in the colonies; the colonials kept their libraries well stocked with books on British impeachment.[13] They drew on more than book learning; the Founding Fathers knew impeachment firsthand from debating the concept in their state legislatures and drafting their state constitutions, which included state impeachment clauses. Colonial writers and practicing lawyers cited British impeachment trials.[14] Thomas Jefferson and other colonial leaders read and relied in particular on British scholar Richard Wooddeson's *Lectures on the Laws of England*, a published "series of highly regarded, well-attended, and widely publicized lectures on the law beginning in 1777."[15]

Wooddeson's theme: Impeachment solves abuses of power hurting the community, which may not be solved in ordinary courts. Explaining centuries of British law and history, Wooddeson provided examples of impeachable offenses against those who "may abuse their delegated powers to the extensive detriment of the community, and at the same time in a manner not properly cognizable before the ordinary tribunals."[16] Wooddeson's examples included impeachment for those who subvert fundamental laws, introduce arbitrary power, and betray trust, and "propound or support pernicious and dishonorable measures . . . to obtain exorbitant grants or incompatible employments . . ."[17]

Although the English Parliament attempted to use impeachment to counter the absolute powers of the king or queen[18] by targeting "fawning favorites" and making political statements against the monarchy's complete authority,[19] such efforts were hamstrung by the absolute ruler of Great Britain—who could dissolve Parliament on a whim.[20]

The Founding Fathers used their knowledge of British impeachment law and their experiences under that ancient law to address many dangers they foresaw with their U.S. leaders, including the following high risks:

1. Presidential incapacity or negligence;
2. Presidential tyranny;
3. Presidential corruption;
4. Betrayal of trust by their president to a foreign power; and
5. An overbroad law of treason, which could be abused by the government to terrorize its citizens and officials by determining "treason" after the fact.

First, Founding Father and future president James Madison stated an "indispensable" need "for defending the community against the incapacity, negligence or perfidy [faithlessness[21]] of the Chief Magistrate" (a title later changed to "President"). Madison was crystal clear: negligence or loss of capacity must be subject to impeachment; he predicted that, with a single executive, loss of capacity or corruption was "within the compass of probable events; and either of them might be fatal to the Republic."[22]

Second, tyranny was a major concern for the colonists, who had included in the Declaration of Independence an impressive and lengthy list of acts of "absolute tyranny" by King George.[23] The Constitution writers had firsthand knowledge of the dangers of abuse of power by the king and the whims and edicts of his governors and minions.[24] The founders' experiences and knowledge of English history raised the "specter of a president swollen with power and grown tyrannical; and fear of presidential abuses prevailed over frequent objections that impeachment threatened his independence."[25] Madison and other Founding Fathers expressed concerns that the chief executive of the United States might be transformed into a monarch.[26]

Third, a great concern expressed by the Founding Fathers was corruption, as James Madison expressed above as potentially fatal to the Republic. Either negligence or corruption can lead to a fourth category—betrayal of trust—also a great concern of the Founding Fathers, including Convention delegate

Gouverneur Morris, the author of the Constitution's Preamble.[27] Morris, initially skeptical of the need for impeachment, conceded he had changed his mind during constitutional debates. Morris bluntly addressed his concern that a president might betray the country by being bribed by a foreign power:

> He may be bribed by a greater interest to betray his trust; and no one would say that we ought to expose ourselves to the danger of seeing the first Magistrate in foreign pay without being able to guard against it by displacing him.[28]

To reinforce his point that even the most wealthy and powerful men could be bribed, Morris reminded his colleagues of a shocking discovery reported in the late seventeenth century: a secret deal concocted for the French king Louis XIV to pay large sums to the British king Charles II. In the 1670 Secret Treaty of Dover, the English king had agreed to assist with the destruction of the Dutch Republic, to someday convert to the Roman Catholic faith, and to cooperate in other concealed arrangements. Gouverneur Morris referred to the scandal as he addressed the vast wealth of one man who virtually held all the land in the kingdom—without limitation, in "fee simple"—greedily betraying his country's trust:

> One would think the King of England well secured against bribery. He has as it were a fee simple in the whole Kingdom. Yet Charles II was bribed by Louis XIV.[29]

Finally, beyond incapacity or negligence, tyranny, corruption, and trust betrayal, the Founding Fathers understood the danger of abusive treason laws. England used changing, flexible concepts of treason to target and kill enemies of the king and his representatives. The broad English treason clause—the "salvo"—allowed a tribunal to determine in retrospect whether conduct was treasonable.[30] English law permitted officials to be impeached before the lords on serious, felony death-penalty charges for treason.[31]

Thus, in 1787, the Founding Fathers came together in Philadelphia at the Constitutional Convention understanding the dangers facing the new nation and prepared to address many concerns, including their future leaders' incapacity or negligence, tyranny, betrayal of trust, and corruption, and great potential for abuse with any overbroad definition of treason. Their solutions and safeguards included granting sole impeachment power to Congress to "bridle" the president[32] with their power of removal, and their ability "to tear down his arbitrary ministers and 'favorites.'"[33]

And, the Americans would directly combat tyrannical tendencies in powerful leaders who could simply dismiss a legislative body by excluding that British practice from the United States Constitution; the framers would give no power to the president to eradicate the body capable of impeaching him, and further, would refuse the president the power to pardon an impeachment.

The new Constitution would prohibit a variety of other potentially tyrannical activities, preventing the president from becoming a king: The president couldn't accept a noble title without permission from Congress; Congress was given the power to override a presidential veto; and special laws targeting groups of people for punishment and laws criminalizing lawful behavior after-the-fact were banned.[34]

Also, in order to avoid the abuses of the overbroad British definition of treason, U.S. constitutional "Treason" would emerge from the Constitutional Convention narrowly defined, with strict rules of evidence written into the Constitution and using phrases borrowed from part of the English law.[35] Constitutional treason would be defined only as levying war against the United States or giving aid and comfort to U.S. enemies.

The framers of the Constitution added a strict rule that no

person could be convicted of treason without two witnesses testifying to the same overt act, or unless the accused person confessed in open court. Here again, the Founding Fathers used ancient British language, but dramatically changed the ancient British law of treason to provide safeguards for anyone accused of it.[36] In fact, the change was so great that, as the key thinkers entered the final September 8, 1787, committee meeting on the Impeachment Clause wording, they realized and then solved a basic, emergent problem: a mainstay of British impeachment—treason—was now so limited in application that it wouldn't be a viable reason for removing badly performing U.S. officials.

THE BIRTH OF THE AMERICAN IMPEACHMENT CLAUSE: SEPTEMBER 8, 1787

Our Impeachment Clause—particularly the language "other high Crimes and Misdemeanors"—was born on September 8, 1787. A "Committee of Eleven" debated an earlier recommendation of a very narrow impeachment clause, with removal from office only for treason and bribery. The framers well knew the importance of every word of the clause as they debated; they recognized they were writing for posterity.[37]

The stage was set to determine if a category should be added for wrongdoing other than treason and bribery. George Mason of Virginia, an important and consistent champion throughout the Convention of the need for impeachment, became a key speaker in this historic debate. Mason fought adamantly for impeachment. He sought earlier in the Convention to advocate for impeachment as a method to minimize the risk of electoral corruption; the fact that voters could make their own choice in reelection would not suffice. Mason had declared that "no point is of more importance" than the retaining of impeachment in the Constitution.[38]

In the final debate of September 8, Mason referenced the British government's ongoing impeachment trial of India Governor-General Hastings, whose alleged wrongdoings would never fit within the U.S. proposed categories of treason and bribery.[39] Using the Hastings case as an example,[40] Mason famously argued that limiting the Impeachment Clause to only bribery and treason "will not reach many great and dangerous offenses." He then moved to add "maladministration," to the impeachment language. James Madison commented on the overbreadth of the word, which would allow the Senate—at their pleasure—to remove an official for any act of maladministration: "So vague a term will be equivalent to a tenure during pleasure of the Senate." Mason withdrew his overbroad term and substituted the phrase "other high crimes and misdemeanors,"[41] the very impeachment language used in the Hastings trial. Thus was born the most fundamental phrase in American impeachment law. But it would not become the supreme law of the land unless and until state ratifying conventions decided to ratify the Constitution.

HISTORIC FIGURES IN THE RATIFICATION OF THE CONSTITUTION AND THE MEANING OF THE IMPEACHMENT CLAUSE

The framers of the Constitution set out to advocate and educate delegates at the state ratifying conventions amid controversy, insults, strong language, and minor mob action. For reasons unrelated to the Impeachment Clause, George Mason was not among the signers of or advocates for adoption of the Constitution,[42] but we know that Mason—the man who gave us the term "high Crimes and Misdemeanors" for U.S. impeachment—knew what he was doing in defending against badly performing officials. He'd led efforts with his friend and neighbor George Washington in Fairfax County to finance, arm, and drill the militia as they prepared for war with Britain. He studied political theory and had given "great thought" to political reconstruction; he and the key Founding Fathers "knew exactly what they were doing." Twenty-first-century historians consider Mason among the well-read Revolutionary-era thinkers studying the "inherently corrupt and conniving character of British government."[43] Mason was the principal author of the Virginia Constitution, which provided for impeachment of the governor for endangering the safety of the state. Mason and Thomas Jefferson started the ball rolling for American independence in May 1774, drafting the resolution denouncing the British blockade of Boston as a "hostile invasion."[44] It was Mason who proposed the Virginia Bill of Rights, the parent of all Bills of Rights, and "one of the greatest liberty documents of all time."[45]

Many of the other Founding Fathers, however, effectively explained and advocated for ratification of the new constitution and its system of government with separation of powers, and checks and balances, including detailed explanations of the purposes, meaning, and uses of the Impeachment Clause. If these advocates had failed, our nation would not exist as we know it.

Importantly for twenty-first-century Americans, the Founding Fathers—deliberately and articulately—preserved evidence of their intent as they explained the Impeachment Clause and other elements of our fundamental documents to their colleagues.

James Wilson of Pennsylvania, for example, provided us with an important record of the Founding Fathers' intent regarding the use and purposes of impeachment, in his 1787 explanation to his state ratifying convention on Congress's check on a president they may impeach for such harmful conduct as negligence or inattention, for his appointments, and for attempting to shift criminality to others. Wilson was an important force in obtaining Pennsylvania's ratification of the Constitution.[46] He reassured the Pennsylvania state ratifying convention in 1787, for which he served as a delegate, of controls on "our President":

The executive power is better to be trusted when it has
no screen. Sir, we have a responsibility in the person of
our President; he cannot act improperly, and hide either
his negligence or inattention; he cannot roll upon any
other person his criminality; no appointment can take
place without his nomination; and he is responsible for
every nomination he makes . . . far from being above the
laws, he is amenable to them in his private character as
a citizen, and in his public character by **impeachment**.
(Emphasis in original.)[47]

As one of six men who signed both the Declaration of
Independence and the Constitution, the influential Wilson
played a major role in the Constitutional Convention in several
matters involving the chief executive. The well-respected
Wilson—"the leading Lawyer of Philadelphia"—made the
motion at the Constitutional Convention that executive power
be vested in a single executive.[48] Wilson's other proposals
included direct election of the president.[49] James Wilson later
served as a Supreme Court Justice and law professor.

Alexander Hamilton, the thirty-year-old New York delegate to the Constitutional Convention, provides us significant
evidence on the Founding Fathers' intent as to the purposes
and uses of impeachment. Hamilton had published accounts
of British abuses as a King's College student in New York and
wrote, post-Convention, of the British antecedents of U.S. impeachment[50] as coauthor (with James Madison and John Jay) of
important essays we read today as *The Federalist Papers*. These
explanatory essays helped to persuade state ratifying conventions to adopt the new Constitution.

Revolutionary War hero Hamilton, who impressed General
Washington with his spectacular artillery work, served also as
Washington's aide-de-camp, lugging around a sack of books
for study between his exploits in the war. An officer claimed
of Hamilton that he thought as well as wrote for Washing-

ton. Hamilton later served President Washington as secretary of the treasury, "a cabinet secretary of tireless virtuosity who would function as his unofficial prime minister."[51] Washington regarded Hamilton as quick in perception, with intuitively great judgment and excelling in whatever he took on.[52] Hamilton explained impeachment to his fellow Americans debating ratification of the Constitution in the classical sense of the word "political," famously stating that impeachment offenses are "political, as they relate chiefly to 'injuries done immediately to the society itself.'"[53]

Hamilton was also remarkably prescient, understanding the important future role of the Senate in impeachment. He wrote passionately and at length in Federalist papers 65 and 66 on the reason for using the Senate—a most deliberative body, most dignified and independent, most likely "to feel confidence enough in its own situation to preserve, unawed and uninfluenced, the necessary impartiality between an individual accused and the representatives of the people [the House], his accusers . . ."—as the final check on impeachment, while the House would have independent responsibility for bringing charges. The Senate was a better choice to judge the matter, Hamilton wrote, emphasizing the advantages of a larger number of persons than a court or jury, finding strength in numbers and the fact that the accused could still be subject to a separate judicial process for criminal prosecution.[54]

The Constitution became effective on June 21, 1788, when New Hampshire became the ninth of the twelve states ratifying. On March 4, 1789, the first Congress under the Constitution convened in New York City. James Madison—who continued to use the word "maladministration" in explaining and providing examples of impeachable conduct[55]—was an active U.S. representative in that first Congress, introducing the proposed Bill of Rights in the House, on June 8, 1789. Through James Madison we have rich information on the intent of the Founding Fathers.[56]

Madison had helped draft Virginia's state constitution in 1776, represented his state in key Revolutionary-era delegations, and helped draft the "Virginia Plan," which laid the groundwork for the Constitutional Convention, where he was a key advocate and valuable reporter. Madison's moniker, "Father of the Constitution," was hard-earned: He worked effectively at the Philadelphia Convention as an advocate for ratification, and with Hamilton and John Jay in writing *The Federalist Papers*. He continued his service as a member of the Virginia ratification convention.[57]

As a member of Congress, Madison spoke passionately on the dangers to our liberties from officials violating the public trust once entrenched in office:

> The danger to liberty, the danger of mal-administration, has not yet been found to lie so much in the facility of introducing improper persons into office, as in the difficulty of displacing those who are unworthy of the public trust.[58]

Congressman Madison spoke in congressional debate on creation of what would become our State Department and on presidential responsibility for his executive officers, arguing that the "wanton removal" of a meritorious officer would amount to impeachable maladministration.[59]

The president's authority to remove subordinates, Madison reasoned, made "[the president], in a peculiar manner, responsible for the conduct" of executive officers. It would, Madison said, "subject him to impeachment himself, if he suffers them to perpetrate with impunity high crimes and misdemeanors against the United States, or neglects to superintend their conduct, so as to check their excesses."[60]

We can take Madison's concerns and words to the bank. Madison was an extraordinary man, even among his great peers. His fellow delegate William Pierce of Georgia explained "every Person seems to acknowledge his greatness . . . From a spirit of industry and application which he possesses in a most eminent degree, he always comes forward the best informed man of any point in debate. The affairs of the United States, he perhaps has the most correct knowledge of, of any man in the Union."[61]

After serving in Congress, Madison served as secretary of state and then as the fourth president of the United States. The last survivor of the constitutional signers, Madison died at age eighty-five in 1836. In his old age, he had succeeded Thomas Jefferson as University of Virginia president and further served his state in developing a new Virginia constitution.[62]

2

LEGAL PRINCIPLES AND PROCESSES

OF IMPEACHMENT

Congress dominates impeachment. The word "sole" appears only twice in the Constitution: in Article I, Section 2, Clause 5, giving the House "sole Power" of impeachment ("The House of Representatives shall chuse their Speaker and other Officers, and shall have the sole Power of Impeachment") and in Article I, Section 3, giving the "sole Power" to the Senate to try impeachment cases:

> The Senate shall have the sole Power to try all Impeachments. When sitting for that Purpose, they shall be on Oath or Affirmation. When the President of the United States is tried, the Chief Justice shall preside: And no Person shall be convicted without the Concurrence of two thirds of the Members present. U.S. Const. Art. I, Sec. 3, Clause 6.

The House investigates and decides whether to "impeach" an official at the first stage of constitutional impeachment. The House may acquire information and trigger an impeachment investigation in any number of ways. Members may discuss charges on the floor or by introducing a resolution. Members may glean information from various sources such as a grand jury or a state legislature, or information from a committee.[63]

If a majority of the House votes to approve any one of the

"Articles of Impeachment"—the charges—then the officer has been "impeached." The impeached officer then faces trial in the United States Senate, which sits as the court and jury.

The Senate has the final say in the impeachment process. The legal word for the "final say" concept is "non-justiciability." This means that the decision is not subject to review by the court system, according to the U.S. Supreme Court. The words of the Constitution's Impeachment Clause "commit the responsibility" in impeachment to the Senate.[64] The Supreme Court has noted that not "a single word in the history of the Constitutional Convention . . . even alludes to the possibility of judicial review in the context of the impeachment powers," while judicial review is available as a check on other legislative powers.[65]

The Supreme Court has confirmed that the language of the Impeachment Clause does not require the Senate to conduct a judicial-style trial; the Senate must only place the senators—who act as jurors—under oath or affirmation, follow the voting rule (two-thirds of members present are required for conviction), and use the chief justice of the Supreme Court to preside. The Senate has developed procedural rules over the centuries, with appointment of a Senate trial committee and streamlining allowing for conduct of other work of government.[66] In a Senate impeachment trial, members of the House of Representatives serve as prosecutors and present the case; they are called "House managers."

The Constitution limits the effect of an impeachment conviction:

> Judgment in Cases of Impeachment shall not extend further than to removal from Office, and disqualification to hold and enjoy any Office of honor, Trust or Profit under the United States: but the Party convicted shall nevertheless be liable and subject to Indictment, Trial, Judgment and Punishment, according to Law. U.S. Const., Art. I, Sec. 3, Clause 7.

The Senate votes on each impeachment article separately, with each article requiring two-thirds voting yes to convict on the article. If the Senate convicts on at least one article of impeachment, removal is automatic.[67] The Senate, if it chooses, may hold a vote to decide separately whether the convicted official is forever barred from holding office. Impeachment in the Senate is thus a special form of trial, a "Chastisement," as Alexander Hamilton put it.

The Constitution permits impeachment of "civil officers of the United States," but provides no definition for them. The Senate has ruled that senators are not "civil Officers" subject to impeachment. The Congressional Research Service bookends the issue by suggesting that any official who is a principal officer—such as a head of an agency, an administrator, or a commissioner—is likely impeachable. A lower-level executive-branch worker—such as a federal employee in the civil service, with no presidential appointment or significant authority—may not be impeachable.[68] We know through impeachment experience that cabinet members are impeachable.

Since no loss of liberty is at stake, and the accused is not subject to criminal penalties, double jeopardy does not apply to impeachment. The Constitution says the accused official—even if already tried in a criminal court for the same bad acts—isn't facing trial two times for the same crime when impeached. Regardless of whether an officer is acquitted or convicted in a criminal proceeding, the impeachment may—and has—gone forward.[69] Alexander Hamilton made clear the framers' intent that the impeached offender could still be criminally charged, independent of impeachment punishment:

> [T]he punishment which may be the consequence of conviction upon impeachment is not to terminate the chastisement of the offender. After having been sentenced to perpetual ostracism from the esteem and con-

fidence and honors and emoluments of his country, he will still be liable to prosecution and punishment in the ordinary course of law.[70]

Hamilton's words and the historical examples of judges convicted in impeachment—running the gamut from judges whose underlying behavior yielded separate criminal conviction, to judges with no capability to form any intent—resolve questions of criminality requirements[71] and processes in impeachment.[72] But debate continues as to whether the president of the United States is so special as to be entitled to immunity from criminal prosecution while in office.[73]

TWENTY-FIRST-CENTURY IMPEACHMENT CASES CONFIRM: NO CRIMINAL INTENT, NO CRIME, AND NO LAW OR CONSTITUTIONAL VIOLATION IS REQUIRED FOR "HIGH CRIMES AND MISDEMEANORS."

Twenty-first-century congressional resolutions and reports[74] repeatedly take pains—especially where the impeachment before them also involves convictions for crime—to clarify the purpose of impeachment: "simply to remove the offender from office" in a noncriminal proceeding;[75] "'high Crimes and Misdemeanors' refers to misconduct that damages the state and the operations of governmental institutions, and is not to be limited to cases of criminal misconduct. The non-criminal process imposes no criminal penalties."[76]

Yet, comments persist implying that impeachment requires a crime or criminal mind-set. Officeholders facing impeachment—and their advocates—in particular might urge that impeachment requires a criminal act for several possible reasons: (1) they want to keep their jobs; (2) they are genuinely confused by the fact that good House prosecutors do indeed make all sorts of charges in an impeachment action, including charging very serious law and crime violations, because they are trying to make the best case possible for bad conduct—including crimes—and are permitted to use "catch-all" articles of impeachment; or (3) they do not know the specifics of American history as it pertains to the colonists taking a British legal tradition and adapting it to their own purposes for a new nation.

While the framers of the Constitution placed limits and rules on officers—barring officeholders from acceptance of such items as foreign gifts, presents, emoluments, or titles unless Congress consents; prohibiting any state from granting any title of nobility;[77] and barring the president from receiving from any state or the United States any increased or decreased compensation during the president's term "or any other Emolument"[78]—Congress is not required to prove a specific, legal, or constitutional-level impropriety for the mainstay impeachment ground of "high Crimes and Misdemeanors." While Congress is allowed to make such claims, impeachment does not require it. Moreover, commission of a crime or breaking the law is not the equivalent of an impeachable offense, as modern Impeachment demonstrates in practice.

Just as Alexander Hamilton defined impeachable offenses as relating "chiefly to injuries done immediately to the society itself,"[79] U.S. congressional staff in their well-respected report on presidential impeachment emphasized the same concept almost two hundred years later: "the crucial factor is not the intrinsic quality of behavior but the significance of its effect upon our constitutional system or the functioning of our government."[80] Harm, regardless of such factors as intent or criminality or breaking a law, is the key.

This concept of harm explains why we place crucial focus on the Founding Fathers' study of ancient British law and the British law lectures of Wooddeson; the men who wrote the Constitution understood the British law–focus on harms of maladministration in using the phrase "high Crimes and Misdemeanors," with the British list of impeachable offenses "as peculiarly injure the Commonwealth" including betrayal of trust, neglect of duty, acting grossly contrary to the duty of his office to carry out oath of office, or obtaining "exorbitant grants or incompatible employments."[81] James Madison was clear that a president could be removed via impeachment for "mal-practice or neglect of duty." The future president bluntly explained impeachment's protection from the danger of a president who might "lose capacity," or "might betray his trust to foreign powers."[82]

The Founding Fathers foresaw impeachment against a president who might "engage in corrupting of electors," concerns expressed by both George Mason and Gouverneur Morris.[83] Thus, impeachment is a congressional process to remove high public officials if they, regardless of motive or even capacity to form intent, pose substantial risk of injury to society.

Judges are the most commonly impeached high officials in the history of the United States. Until the latter part of the twentieth century, confusion reigned in various minds as to whether judges and other civil officers were held to different standards. It's now well accepted—including in House of Representatives management of presidential impeachment—that the constitutional standard of "high Crimes and Misdemeanors" applies to both judges and executive branch officers.[84]

Federal judges, including Supreme Court justices, are subject to impeachment as a result of Article III of the Constitution, which vests the "Judicial Power of the United States . . . in one supreme Court, and in such inferior Courts as the Congress may from time to time ordain and establish."[85]

While federal judges hold their offices "during good Behavior" under the Constitution,[86] "good Behavior" is not the impeachment standard; indeed, the Constitutional Convention rejected any impeachment standard other than "high Crimes and Misdemeanors" for judges and other civil officers of the United States.[87] In 1974, the House Judiciary Committee's impeachment inquiry investigated whether the "good behavior" clause provided an additional ground for impeachment of judges, and concluded "[i]t does not." The House report on the impeachment of President Clinton agreed: impeachable conduct for judges mirrored impeachable conduct for other civil officers in the government.[88]

Moreover, while officers of the executive branch and the Judicial Branch are evaluated by the same standard[89] ("Treason, Bribery, and other high Crimes and Misdemeanors"), the Majority Staff in the Clinton presidential impeachment understood that the nature of a president's duties (for example, as head of the Department of Justice, the federal government's prosecutorial authority charged with taking care that the laws are faithfully executed) rendered the president's special constitutional duty at least as high as a judge's.[90]

Two constitutional clauses are crucial to understanding the president's responsibilities:

> [The President] shall take Care that the laws be faithfully executed . . . U.S. Const. Art. II, Sec. 3.

> "I do solemnly swear (or affirm) that I will faithfully execute the Office of President of the United States, and will to the best of my Ability preserve, protect, and defend the Constitution of the United States." U.S. Const. Art. II, Sec. 1, Clause 8.

In 1974, the impeachment inquiry staff report of the House of Representatives concluded that these two clauses represent three distinct responsibilities on the part of the president:

1. "To take care that the laws be faithfully executed";
2. "To faithfully execute the Office of President of the United States"; and
3. "To preserve, protect, and defend the Constitution of the United States."

Of the first two duties, the staff report explained:

> A President must carry out the obligations of his office diligently and in good faith. The "take care" duty emphasizes the responsibility of a President for the overall conduct of the executive branch, which the Constitution vests in him alone.

> He must take care that the executive is so organized and operated that this duty is performed.

Of the third duty, the House staff report concluded in 1974:

> The duty of a president to "preserve, protect and defend the Constitution" to the best of his abilities includes the duty not to abuse his powers or transgress their limits—not to violate the rights of citizens such as guaranteed by the Bill of Rights, which the Constitution vests in him alone, and not to act in derogation of powers vested elsewhere in the Constitution."[91]

Violation of a duty subjects executive branch officers to impeachment. That violation of duty need not be a crime. The House Judiciary Committee has observed:

> The House and Senate have both interpreted the phrase "other high Crimes and Misdemeanors" broadly, finding that impeachable offenses need not be limited to criminal conduct. Congress has repeatedly defined "other high Crimes and Misdemeanors" to be serious violations of the public trust, not necessarily indictable under criminal laws.[92]

Thus, in reading charges in U.S. impeachment cases, you will frequently find noncriminal claims that public officials violated their duties or oath or seriously undermined public confidence in their ability to perform their official functions.[93]

Article II of the U.S. Constitution lists many significant presidential duties, apart from the president's oath and "take care" duties.[94] Article II, Section 2, lists the president's responsibilities as commander in chief: obtaining advice and consent for treaties, nominating a variety of officers (for whom, we have seen in Founding Father statements, the president is responsible), and pardon power. Article II, Section 3, of the Constitution lists presidential obligations to deliver a report on the "State of the Union," receive ambassadors and other public ministers, and commission officers. Presidential abuse, neglect, or violation of presidential duties and powers subjects the president to impeachment, as the framers stated and impeachment cases demonstrate. One abuse of power not yet involved in a case of House Impeachment is the Presidential power to pardon.

Article II, Section 2, Clause 1, of the Constitution allows presidential pardons "except in Cases of Impeachment":

> [The President] . . . shall have Power to grant Reprieves and Pardons for Offenses against the United States, except in Cases of Impeachment. U.S. Const. Art. II, Sec. 2, Clause 1.

This clause protects congressional sole power to impeach—and make it stick. Congress may overcome a presidential veto of an Act of Congress in Article I, Section 7,[95] but the president is given no chance to overcome congressional impeachment. While presidents cannot pardon their own—or anyone's—impeachment, debate remains as to whether they can pardon their own criminality. Most scholars—aside from lawyers defending a president—would agree that the Constitution would prohibit such an outrageous act; "a man should not be a judge in his own case," we are a nation of laws, not men, and "the

President is not above the law." The Supreme Court described and reinforced the Founding Fathers' intent: the pardoning power was intended to commute sentences on conditions which do not, in themselves, offend the Constitution . . ."[96]

A pardon can prevent criminal prosecution, but a pardon cannot prevent impeachment; impeachment is not a criminal process.

To date, no president has been impeached for abuse of his pardoning power, but the Founding Fathers discussed the issue and impeachable concepts beyond pardon power in regard to "sheltering suspicious persons." At the Virginia ratifying convention, George Mason worried that the president might use his pardoning power to "pardon crimes which were advised against himself" or before indictment or conviction "to stop inquiry and prevent detection." James Madison responded to the concern with a very broad answer, extending impeachment beyond pardon abuse: "[I]f the President be connected, in any suspicious manner, with any person, and there be grounds to believe he will shelter him, the House of Representatives can impeach him; they can remove him if found guilty . . ."[97]

Legal writers have offered theoretical examples of pardon abuses which may be impeachable, including presidential attempts to pardon a horrible offense before its commission, which would, in effect, grant a president the power to waive any law, as to any person.[98] Such examples of gross abuse of presidential power demonstrate understanding that the crucial factor in impeachment for high crimes and misdemeanors is not the motive or intent of the president in granting a pardon, but rather the "substantial effect" of abusive pardon activity: we would become a lawless nation.[99]

We owe much of our modern understanding of impeachment and the importance of the "substantial effect" of malfunctioning officials to the 1974 House Committee on the Judiciary investigating President Nixon's conduct, which commissioned an impeachment inquiry staff report summarizing the history of impeachment, the phrase "high Crimes and Misdemeanors," and congressional grounds, emphasizing history, duty, substantiality of harm, and the intent of the Founding Fathers. Congress does not plead impeachment as difficult-to-prove constitutional treason or bribery.[100] The House managers intelligently plead treachery, corruption, and financial misconduct as "high Crimes and Misdemeanors" or "impeachable offenses," avoiding the more difficult-proof elements of "Treason" or "Bribery."[101]

In charging U.S. officers in impeachment, Congress pleads intentional misconduct and unintentional maladministration. House managers may combine allegations requiring lesser proof with intentional and criminal misconduct. Separate articles of impeachment may reword and repeat, generalize and aggregate, and use "catch-all" clauses. In other words, prosecutors use tactics to draft the allegations in order to get the votes needed for impeachment conviction.

The 1974 staff report provides the following items, numbered 1 through 5 (headings have been added here), generally categorizing the nature of impeachments (up to 1974) and emphasizing the key concepts of "significant effect" and the effect of scope of duty on impeachment liability. The frequently cited 1974 report explained that such a list would necessarily be nonexhaustive.

1. **Poaching.** Exceeding constitutional bounds of the powers of the office in derogation of the powers of another branch;[102]
2. **Gross conduct.** Behaving in a manner grossly incompatible with the proper function and purpose of the office;
3. **Abuse of office.** Employing the office for an improper purpose or for personal gain;
4. **Violations of duty.** Impeachment grounds derive from understanding the nature, function, and duties of the office;
5. **Damage significance.** "The crucial factor is not the

intrinsic quality of behavior but the significance of its effect upon our constitutional system or the functioning of government."[103]

We continue to study, explain, and supplement these broad, nonexhaustive categories in the twenty-first century, drawing on the words of Founding Fathers, relevant British impeachment law, and congressional actions in each of the U.S. impeachment cases, including significant post-1974 impeachment activity. In nearly a quarter of a millennia since the Constitution was ratified, Congress has impeached and brought to trial nineteen persons; six of those nineteen impeachments occurred since the 1974 report was issued. Of the total (eight) U.S. impeachment *convictions* in U.S. history, one-half (four) have occurred from 1986 to this writing.

The following continuation—also a nonexhaustive and more specific list—provides more details of impeachable maladministration, with the overarching consideration—the key component in U.S. impeachment, as always—the substantial effect of the maladministration:

1. Acting to defeat claims of the United States;[104]
2. Acting to shelter or in "connection with, in any suspicious manner with any person and there be grounds to believe the President might shelter him," including pardon abuse;[105]
3. Betraying trust (generally);[106] (to foreign powers);[107]
4. Abuse of office for violations of rights, personal financial gain, embezzlement;[108] (corruption, for personal gain);[109] (to commit sexual assault);[110] depredations (attacking or plundering), which abuse or violate the public trust;[111]
5. Agency/employer liability as principal for persons under control:[112] liability as principal for negligence or inattention; improper acts or attempts to "roll off" criminality on another, including responsibility for agent selection and nominations;[113] failure to make proper appointments or properly

do the work oneself; and responsibility for wrongful firing if merit of the fired person justifies retention;[114]

6. Concealing evidence;[115] obstruction of justice;[116]

7. Conflicts of interest; pecuniary inducement;[117]

8. Corruption in elections;[118]

9. Corruption: in relationships; patterns of behavior; corrupt financial relationship at time of nomination or while office holder[119] (prior to federal office holding or nomination remains open question);[120]

10. Fraud unrelated to duties of office (in tax filings) (in bankruptcy filings);[121]

11. Ignorance: ("too ignorant to perform duties");[122]

12. Lying, perfidy (faithlessness), treachery, disloyalty, deceits, violation of a promise or vow; obstruction of justice, perjury or subornation of perjury;[123] self-dealing;[124] depriving the public of right to honest services of the office;[125] corruption of judicial process;[126] bringing administration of justice into disrepute;[127] conduct harming the public respect and confidence;[128] undermining public confidence in the integrity and impartiality of the administration of justice;[129]

13. Misconduct in "matters outside official duties";[130]

14. Negligence;[131]

15. Revealing confidential information (wiretap);[132]

16. Tyranny and oppression;[133] subverting fundamental laws, introducing arbitrary power; supporting pernicious and dishonorable measures;[134]

17. Unworthy conduct;[135]

18. Violating oath of office and duties;[136] failure to provide Senate "every material intelligence he receives"; giving false information to the Senate; concealing important intelligence that the officer ought to have communicated; failure to provide information in nomination process;[137]

19. Violating court order.[138]

3

FEDERAL IMPEACHMENTS IN THE UNITED STATES

Congress has conducted many impeachment investiga-tions stopping short of impeachment, to important ef-fect, some of which led to no action and others prompting resignation.[139] Most famously, the impeachment investigation of President Richard Nixon was stopped short of a House vote by the president's resignation, after the House Judiciary Com-mittee recommended articles of impeachment.

Congress has taken sixteen impeachment matters from House impeachment to Senate verdict. Those cases involved two presidents, one senator, one secretary of war, and twelve judges. The list: Senator Blount, Judge Pickering, Justice Chase, Judge Peck, Judge Humphreys, President Andrew John-son, Secretary of War Belknap, Judge Swayne, Judge Archbald, Judge Louderback, Judge Ritter, Judge Claiborne, Judge Hast-ings, Judge W. Nixon, President Clinton, and Judge Porteous. Of these sixteen, eight U.S. officers—all federal judges—were both impeached by the House of Representatives and con-victed in the Senate. The list of eight convicted judges were Pickering, Humphreys, Archbald, Ritter, Claiborne, Hast-ings, W. Nixon, and Porteous.[140] Three judicial impeachments (Judges Delahay, English, and Kent) made their way to the Senate; each ended due to resignation.

Each of the nineteen formal impeachments, and other im-portant impeachment activity in U.S. history, deserves study; the circumstances (i.e., successful or unsuccessful prosecution, procedures, duties of the civil officer involved, grounds, and strategy) all provide guidance for maintaining and protecting our democracy. Chief justice of the United States Supreme Court William Rehnquist taught that impeachment activities provide important contributions to law and history—as important as court cases by any court. Rehnquist, the sixteenth chief justice of the U.S. Supreme Court, prior to presiding over the impeachment trial of President Clinton, authored a book about two significant impeachment trials and commented on the House impeachment investigation of President Richard Nixon that led to President Nixon's resignation, halting the House impeachment activity. The chief justice explained:

> The impeachment acquittals of Justice Chase and President Johnson—"cases" decided not by the courts but by the United States Senate—surely contributed as much to the maintenance of our tripartite federal system of government as any case decided by any court.[141]

Below are the nineteen impeachments, plus other significant impeachment activity in our history.

Senator William Blount
Date of final Senate action: January 11, 1799
Result: expelled from Senate for "High Misdemeanor"—impeachment charges dismissed

The first U.S. impeachment trial arose from a Senator's grandiose plans to foment war and thwart U.S. stated foreign and domestic policy. Senator William Blount was a land-speculating, securities-peddling swindler who sought to benefit his real estate holdings by seizing the Floridas and Louisianas for Great Britain and to incite the Creek and Cherokee nations to war.

Handsome, born to great wealth, and seemingly sincere,

Blount "was more interested in what his country could do for him than what he could do for his country."[142] To avoid dangerous fighting, Blount's father procured a paymaster position for Blount during the American Revolution, which he misused to add to his fortune.[143] The land-speculating Blount ultimately acquired millions of acres of western land throughout his career in office-holding, a career he spent in attempts to stimulate settlement to his lands.

The charming swindler spent time in the 1780s bilking Revolutionary-era investors out of redeemable securities and acquiring more western lands. Blount's long, varied political career previewed the later treachery that brought about his impeachment. He was elected from North Carolina as a Constitutional Convention delegate, arriving to the historic Convention a month late (on June 20, 1787). By July 1787, Blount had violated the Constitutional Convention's rule of secrecy by sending copies of the draft Constitution to North Carolina contacts, planning "not many years hence [we] be separated and distinct governments perfectly independent of each other."[144] He stayed at the Convention only two weeks, returning to New York where he advertised his western lands while serving in Congress. Blount returned to the Constitutional Convention to see the final draft finished and to be shown as a signer of the U.S. Constitution.

After many political ups and downs, Blount's friends in Congress persuaded President Washington to appoint him governor of Tennessee territory, where he moved in 1790. The new Governor swore in twenty-three-year-old Andrew Jackson as attorney general. Convinced statehood would bring more value to his huge holdings, Blount convened a state convention in January 1796, after which he was elected senator. In June 1796, Tennessee entered the Union.[145]

Senator Blount's impeachment-causing wrongdoing came during a time of great vulnerability for the United States. In the twenty years following the Declaration of Independence, President Washington achieved the U.S. stated foreign-policy goal of neutrality through diplomacy, shows of force, the pardons power, payments, and outright war; Washington managed to achieve peace with France, England, Spain, moonshiners, and Native Americans,[146] bringing about what historians call "the last phase of the War for Independence."[147] Peace for the United States, however, didn't translate into peace in Europe, where wars prevented cross-Atlantic flow of immigrants to Blount's lands.[148] Land values plummeted, ruining Blount. Only senatorial immunity prevented Blount's jailing for his debts. His schemes aiming to drive settlers to his western lands blossomed into stirring war in Spanish and French colonies in Florida and Louisiana using a variety of methods, including soldiers of fortune and a U.S. Indian Agent, inciting native Americans against nearby settlers.[149]

On July 3, 1797, President John Adams forwarded documents to Congress exposing the treachery of Blount, who, with soldier of fortune John Chisholm and fellow land speculator Nicholas Romayne, had made plans to violate the American law of neutrality and foment war with Spain and then France for the benefit of Great Britain via incitement of Native Americans.[150]

Blount's impeachment reflects a complex procedural history: On July 7, 1797, the House voted to impeach Blount and asked a member to go to the Senate "and at the bar thereof" explain that the House would, "in due course," provide articles of impeachment. The Senate did not wait for articles of impeachment, instead hearing evidence—from its own members—contradicting Blount's denials and identifying Blount's handwriting on correspondence revealing his plans. The full Senate "expelled" their fellow Senator,[151] having found him guilty of a "high misdemeanor inconsistent with his public trust and duty."[152]

Blount returned to Knoxville in September 1797, still well liked by his constituents, escorted as a hero by the city's founder and speaker of the state House of Representatives. He declined requests to run for reelection; his friend Andrew Jackson was elected to fill his office.[153] Blount went on to serve in the state Senate, chosen speaker of that body.[154]

Six months after expulsion, a House committee reported out articles of impeachment, and the Senate then sat as a high court of impeachment in Philadelphia. Blount was not present; the Senate sergeant at arms, entertained lavishly at home in Knoxville by Blount, accepted Blount's polite refusal to attend.[155]

The debate at the Senate impeachment trial in January 1799 on what was a high crime and misdemeanor was unresolved by the Senate; Senator Blount's formidable lawyers successfully persuaded the Senate—with claims that a senator was not a "civil officer" and that an already-expelled officer was not impeachable—to dismiss the charges in January 1799.[156]

Blount died at his Knoxville mansion in March 1800, ill from overwork after caring for his malaria-stricken wife, mother-in-law, and three of his children.[157]

KEY LESSONS FROM THE BLOUNT CASE

- Fomenting war and interfering with the foreign policies of the United States were regarded and pled by the eighteenth-century House managers, not as "Treason," but as falling within "high Crimes and Misdemeanors"; and the Senate regarded the treachery as "high Misdemeanor" in expulsion.

- Congress needed rules and orderly processes for the House to conduct impeachment and to coordinate trial with the Senate; otherwise, impeached officers would take advantage and hope for errors, inaction, and delay, as clever defense lawyers will seize on procedural errors in obtaining dismissals.

- In its first use, American impeachment carried no criminal trappings; Blount went home to his family and life after his impeachment and expulsion and never returned for the second trial.

Judge John Pickering
Date of final Senate action: March 12, 1804
Result: guilty, removed from office

John Pickering was a respected draftsman of the New Hampshire Constitution and an advocate for the ratification of the U.S. Constitution. He served New Hampshire as a state judge, and then served his country as a federal judge.[158] By 1803, Judge Pickering was senile—incompetent—but remained on the federal bench, wielding tremendous power. He abused the rights of people who appeared in his court, and he could not follow law or basic required procedures, in clear violation of his duties as judge. Judge Pickering was impeached in the House of Representatives and convicted in the Senate of "high Crimes and Misdemeanors." The sad, significant, blunders of the once respected but mentally compromised Judge Pickering—incapable owing to disease of forming an intent to do wrong—were the factual underpinnings of the first impeachment and conviction in the United States.[159]

The impeachment articles included charges of illegally handing over a valuable ship and cargo belonging to the United States to a man who, claiming ownership in court, had no legal claim to the vessel or its contents. The judge denied the U.S. Attorney the right to put on his case with witnesses or to appeal the judge's rulings. The charges also included a variety of intentional acts, but because the judge was conceded "insane," intent could not be proven. Thus, Judge Pickering's impeachment did not require intent; rather, it stemmed from the effect of his unintentional conduct. The impeachment articles included the following allegations:

• Serious injury to the system of justice by, for example, denying lawyers and their client, the United States of America, their legal rights to put on witnesses and appeal decisions, and by having U.S. property illegally seized and given to someone else;

- Absence of temperance and sobriety, and appearing to be in a state of total intoxication on the bench; and

- "Other high misdemeanors . . . degrading to the honor and dignity of the United States."[160] The judge did not appear at his impeachment trial. Judge Pickering's son submitted petitions indicating the judge was "insane" and had been "deranged" for some time.[161] Judge Pickering was found guilty of "high Crimes and Misdemeanors" and removed from office in March 1804.

Confusion had reigned—and continued for years—as to whether impeachment required a violation of law and whether the proceeding was "criminal," with questions regarding the judge's absence and how to handle his mental state. Critics, confused as to the purpose of impeachment and imbuing the proceeding with criminal trial qualities, believed the trial unfair—as well as politicized—when measured by criminal law standards.[162]

Pickering is consistent with Hamilton's often-used description and understanding that all impeachments are noncriminal processes but "political"[163] (in the sense that the question is whether the high public official is causing substantial injury to society).[164] The most literary of critics conceded that the lack of "responsibility" in Judge Pickering did not render Congress incapable of removing him "for the good of the public service."[165]

The Founding Fathers anticipated the exact problem posed by Judge Pickering's condition and were clear in their intention that impeachment and removal was appropriate where officers—including the president of the United States—lacked legal capacity.[166] Other constitutional provisions for acting on the problem of an officer who lacks capacity do not affect the Impeachment Clause and the provision of sole impeachment powers granted to the House and Senate.[167]

KEY LESSONS FROM THE PICKERING CASE

- The Pickering facts and result support modern congressional embrace of the Founding Fathers' intent by demonstrating that no intent for wrongdoing is required for impeachment for "high Crimes and Misdemeanors."

- The Pickering procedures, trial, and penalty (removal from office) emphasize the difference between a Senate impeachment trial and criminal court; impeachment conviction carries only two possible penalties (removal, and disqualification from future office holding). No loss of liberty was at stake, and Judge Pickering's conviction in impeachment did not result in any criminal penalty.[168]

- The Pickering outcome demonstrates that protection of society is the goal of impeachment. Although the officer's sincere inability to understand or modify his behavior may elicit great sympathy, these facts increase the prospect for future harm if sympathy wins over protecting society.[169]

Justice Samuel Chase
Date of final Senate action: March 1, 1805
Result: not guilty

On the heels of Judge Pickering's conviction, the House impeached U.S. Supreme Court Justice Samuel Chase, an extraordinarily active patriot during the Revolution, delegate to the First Continental Congress, and signer of the Declaration of Independence.[170] Chase was an outspoken fellow and known to speak his mind with "shocking" force.[171] He served in the federal and state legislatures, but opposed ratification of the Constitution. He became a state judge and then was appointed to the U.S. Supreme Court. Loyal to George Washington, Chase switched from anti-Federalist to strident Federalist, "intemperate in his partisanship for the Federalist cause."[172]

Chase's impeachment was prompted by a politicized grand jury charge that he delivered, which inspired an angry President Thomas Jefferson to write to his political lieutenants in the House of Representatives for action.[173] Specifically, Chase severely criticized Jefferson and the Republicans for their attack on the then-recent Supreme Court decision of *Marbury v. Madison* (a case famously asserting and cementing the power of the Supreme Court, the judicial branch, to review actions of Congress, the legislative branch, for constitutionality). An angry President Jefferson asked whether the attack by Chase should "go unpunished."[174]

The lengthy impeachment charges against Chase complained of behavior "highly arbitrary, oppressive and unjust," and "manifest injustice, partiality and intemperance." The House criticized specifics of his rulings, procedures, and opinions in significant detail. But the attack on his judicial practices was capped by Article VIII, the true reason for the impeachment: a complaint of his "intemperate and inflammatory political harangue," in an attempt to "pervert his official right and duty to address the grand jury."[175]

What extreme views—on both sides—brought the House managers and the Republican Senate leader William Giles into the impeachment trial against Chase in the Senate! Vice President Aaron Burr presided. Senator Giles told John Quincy Adams, who would have required "evil intent" for an impeachment,[176] that impeachable conduct need not be criminal or corrupt. All that Giles would require for impeachment was mere disagreement with a decision of the Supreme Court. Giles sought to convict Chase for his "dangerous opinions."[177]

Each side continued their extreme positions, the House managers arguing that a difference in political philosophy or opinion was impeachable: ". . . an impeachable offense could be nothing more than a difference of opinion or political philosophy between a holder of public office and the majority party in Congress."[178]

Chase and his defense team argued that criminal intent was required, even though the recent Pickering case had resulted in a conviction for impeachment where "no criminal conduct had even been alleged," and that Judge Pickering was incapable of forming intent to do wrong.[179]

In his book *Grand Inquests*, Supreme Court Chief Justice Rehnquist used nineteenth-century criteria and practices to demonstrate in point-by-point detail that, while Chase may have been impatient, overbearing, and at times arrogant, he was nonetheless justice-seeking.[180] The wrongs attributed to Justice Chase, so painstakingly analyzed by the chief justice in his book, appear to have resulted in no miscarriage of justice "as it was understood at that time";[181] the claims were not worthy of impeachment.[182]

The significance of Justice Rehnquist's scholarly defense and conclusion is that it emphasizes the most important criteria for impeachment: Is there harm to society? Chase had not engaged in miscarriage of justice in his rulings or in his statements to the grand jury.[183] Justice Rehnquist defended Chase's statements in historical perspective; the criticisms to the grand jury that had so angered President Jefferson were consistent with practices at the time.[184] As modern Chief Justice Rehnquist delicately explained history:

> . . . as the party of Jefferson and Madison moved into avowed opposition to the policies followed by the administration of John Adams, some grand-jury charges took on a more partisan flavor."[185]

On March 1, 1805, the Senate acquitted Justice Chase, who remained in office. The rough and coarse Chase, before his death, had endeared himself to his successor on the Supreme Court, Justice Joseph Story, who commented on Chase's "tenderness of heart."[186] Congress, wisely, did not take on President Jefferson's next suggestion for impeachment: Chief Justice John Marshall.[187]

KEY LESSONS FROM THE CHASE CASE

- The case result vindicated Alexander Hamilton's faith in the Senate as the responsible body for the trial of impeachment, demonstrating the wisdom of the Founding Fathers in placing the trial of impeached officials in the hands of the Senate. Hamilton wrote extensively in Federalist papers 65 and 66 lauding the Senate's suitability for impeachment given its numbers, and advantages over use of the Supreme Court as a deliberative body. Chief Justice Rehnquist praised the process.[188]

- The failure of the prosecution strategy represented what Chief Justice Rehnquist hoped and believed was the end of abuse of impeachment as a method to attack the judicial philosophy of a judge; impeachment of a judge is not a proper weapon for Congress (prompted by the president or not) to resolve philosophical conflicts.

- The failure of the prosecution to demonstrate harm to society reveals the inadequacy of an impeachment predicated on a pretext, assumption of harm, or mere "harangues"; the supposed injustices did not rise to a level of impeachable "high Crimes and Misdemeanors."

Judge James H. Peck
Date of final Senate action: January 31, 1831
Result: not guilty

After attempts in 1826 and 1828 to bring articles of impeachment against the federal judge James Peck, the House finally—in 1830—impeached the judge for his contempt order
imprisoning (for twenty-four hours) and suspending (for
eighteen months) the law license of Luke Lawless, under the
"pretences" of a contempt proceeding, in apparent retalia-
tion for Lawless publishing an article highly critical of Judge
Peck.[189]

The House utilized only one article of impeachment for
abuse of judicial authority and subversion of liberty, a "High
Misdemeanor in Office." The House charged Judge Peck with
acting "unjustly, oppressively, and arbitrarily."[190]

The prosecution and defense took extreme positions, all
of which were inconsistent with the intent of the Founding
Fathers. One House manager argued that "any official act,
committed or omitted by a judge, which is in violation of
the condition of his office, is an impeachable offense under
the Constitution."[191] Judge Peck argued that impeachment
required an illegal act and wrongful intent. His acquittal in
the Senate might best be explained by the House's inability to
demonstrate a sufficiently substantial injury. [192]

KEY LESSON FROM THE PECK CASE

• The 1830 Peck impeachment result may reflect Senate
concerns—beyond confusion on wrongful intent already
rejected as a requirement in Pickering—over whether an
officer's maladministration has a "substantial" effect on
society, particularly one involving an officer's single abuse
of power (in this case, "abuse of judicial authority" and
"subversion of the liberty of the people"[193]). Peck seems to

be a case where societal impact was insufficient and the Senate chose not to exercise its vast impeachment power.

Judge West H. Humphreys
Date of final Senate action: June 26, 1862
Result: guilty, removed from office, and disqualified from thereafter holding any office of honor, trust, or profit under the United States

Impeachment returned as an issue in the buildup to the Civil War, when the abolitionist movement took the center of the political stage.[194] Slavery was the only true issue in the 1856 presidential election,[195] and after Minnesota and Oregon entered the Union in 1858 and 1859, the United States tallied eighteen free states and fifteen slave states. By the 1860 election, Republican candidate Abraham Lincoln faced three opponents but carried every free state, amassing 180 electoral votes. With the election of President Lincoln, extremists whipped up hostilities, praising slavery on the floor of Congress and Southern leaders' serious prophesies of a tropical, Confederate Empire that promised to eliminate world poverty and dominate trade with South America, Europe, and across the Atlantic and the Pacific—based on black enslavement. The Civil War erupted in 1861.[196]

In 1862, Judge West Humphreys, a federal district judge in Tennessee, left his court to accept a judicial appointment in the Confederacy. He failed to resign his United States federal judgeship.

Humphreys' treachery as a federal judge was overwhelming: he publicly advocated secession, revolt, and rebellion; agreed to an act of secession; organized armed rebellion against the United States and levied war against it; conspired to oppose the United States; refused to hold court; acted as a judge for the Confederacy; and unlawfully arrested and imprisoned U.S. citizens. This behavior was charged not as "Treason" but as "High Misdemeanors in Office."[197]

While Judge Humphreys, busy levying war against the United States, did not appear for trial, his failure to appear was no barrier to his conviction on all charges, except the apparently unproven factual claim of confiscation of the property of one Andrew Johnson and one John Catron.[198]

The Senate convicted Judge Humphreys in Impeachment on June 26, 1862. In addition to removal from office, Judge Humphreys was also disqualified from thereafter holding any office of honor, trust, or profit under the United States.[199]

KEY LESSONS FROM THE HUMPHREYS CASE

- Impeachment under "high Crimes and Misdemeanors" requires no proof of intent. As with Judge Pickering, there was never an issue of intent put into evidence at the trial of Judge Humphreys, according to accounts of the trial; Judge Humphreys' motives were not even raised at trial.[200]

- Treachery is pled as "high Crimes and Misdemeanors" and not as treason. The House impeachment charging Judge Humphreys never undertook to plead or prove constitutional treason, instead using phrases such as "regardless of his duties" as a U.S. citizen and "unmindful of his duties" of his office, factually stating effects and outcomes ("he unlawfully arrested and imprisoned US citizens").[201] By charging treachery and treasonous activity in failure to perform his duties—not as treason, but rather as "high Misdemeanors" and "high Crimes and Misdemeanors"[202] the House managers avoided any higher burdens of proof associated with "Treason."

President Andrew Johnson
Date of final Senate action: May 16–26, 1868
Result: not guilty

After President Lincoln's assassination in April 1865,[203] South-
erner Andrew Johnson emerged suddenly as president and
faced what would be bitter Reconstruction after the Civil
War.[204] President Johnson's assertions of control over his cabinet would ultimately lead to his impeachment in the House,
to be tried in a Republican-dominated Senate that held "in its
hands the fate of Andrew Johnson in the same way that the
Jeffersonian Republicans in the Senate had held in their hands
the fate of Samuel Chase."[205]

President Lincoln had hoped for an orderly Reconstruction and restoration of the Southern states' "proper practical
relation" with the Union, but recognized the great difficulties
of implementing a plan of Reconstruction—a "pernicious ab-
straction"—at the time of his last speech, April 11, 1865.[206] Lincoln's Reconstruction plans included recognizing loyal state
governments organized as soon as 10 percent of voters swore
allegiance, and using the congressionally created Freedmen's
Bureau to provide relief to refugees. The work progressed under Johnson through 1865, with the new president appointing
civil governors in those states where Lincoln had not done so.[207]

Nonetheless, restored state governments determined to undermine the Emancipation Proclamation, led by certain former leaders of the Confederacy, complicated matters as "Black
Codes" and other discriminatory badges of inferiority and
second-class citizenship thwarted protection, education, or aid
for the freed slaves.

At the same time, Radical Republicans harbored and voiced
massive policy disagreements with the new president over
how to bring the South back into the Union.[208]

Having suffered verbal and physical abuse from their Southern colleagues in Congress, many Republicans fervently wanted the South to pay a more punitive, higher price; "they resolved to be stern, if not vindictive, toward the vanquished enemy."[209] Race riots in Memphis and New Orleans ensued, resulting in the murders of hundreds of blacks. The Congress elected in 1866 and meeting in 1867 was "in a vindictive temper."[210]

President Johnson, a Democrat possessing an "intense, almost morbidly sensitive pride," was determined to assert his presidential authority in these difficult times. Facing "the most difficult burden imaginable thrust upon him by Lincoln's death," Johnson wished to use his powers of appointment to fill his cabinet—and other offices—with his choices. He had alienated the cabinet he'd inherited from Lincoln with specific actions, such as vetoing the Civil Rights Act, drafted to render the Black Codes inoperative.[211] Moreover, Johnson's heritage, politics, and rhetoric—"haranguing"—drew him further into conflict with the Republican Senate. The clashes grew to open warfare with Congress, which passed a series of laws aimed at tying the new president's hands in his Reconstruction policies, including a "Tenure of Office Act" that prevented the president from removing federal officials whose appointment required Senate confirmation.[212] The president could suspend, but not remove, members of his own cabinet, rendering him "a mere chairman of a cabinet responsible to Congress."[213] Congress overrode Johnson's veto of the Tenure of Office Act.[214]

After Johnson removed cabinet secretary of war Edwin Stanton, ally of the Radical Republicans, the House impeached the president, including two articles charging him with interfering and attempting to set aside Congress's rightful authority; and bringing Congress into reproach, disrepute, and contempt by "harangues" that criticized and questioned the legislative body.

The United States Senate 2017 website tells the story of the Senate trial, declaring it "influential:"[215]

Johnson's Senate trial began on March 5, 1868, operating under newly revised rules and procedures. On May 16, after weeks of tense and dramatic proceedings, the Senate took a test vote on Article XI, a catch-all charge thought by the House managers most likely to achieve a conviction. The drama of the vote has become legendary. With 36 votes for "guilty" needed to constitute a two-thirds majority for conviction, the roll call produced 35 votes for "guilty" and 19 votes for "not guilty." Seven Republicans, known as the "Republican Recusants," joined the 12 Democrats in supporting Johnson. Ten days later, a vote on two more articles produced the same results. To head off further defeats, the Radical Republicans moved to adjourn the trial *sine die*, abruptly ending the impeachment trial of President Andrew Johnson.[216]

The U.S. Senate website explains that this impeachment trial achieved more than saving the president from removal; the Johnson Senate trial strengthened the independence of the executive.[217] The seven Republican senators who voted for acquittal risked and sacrificed their political futures; all were denounced. One of the seven died shortly afterward, and five of the seven were defeated in their next election. President John F. Kennedy regarded the story of Republican senator Edmund Ross, whose principled votes for acquittal ensured the defeat of Ross in his next election and ended his career, as one of Kennedy's "Profiles in Courage."[218] In his analysis of three of the seven Republican Recusants, Chief Justice Rehnquist also recognized the senators' courage to vote their conscience, with valid reasons for acquittal.[219]

KEY LESSONS FROM THE JOHNSON CASE

- The Senate trial fulfilled Hamilton's prediction that the Senate would be the best deliberative body to handle an impeachment trial. Even with modernized procedural efforts, test votes, and conglomerated charges in a "catch-all" provision to appeal to a variety of potential conviction votes, Johnson was acquitted.[220]

- The acquittal prevented Radical Republicans—including Senator Sumner, who viewed impeachment not as a U.S. constitutional impeachment trial but as a vote of confidence under the British parliamentary system[221]—from co-opting the Impeachment Clause. Rehnquist analogized the attitude of Sumner to that of Senator William Giles, who, according to John Quincy Adams, said shortly before the Chase trial that impeachment meant "We want your offices for the purpose of giving them to men who will fill them better."[222] Thus, the Senate rose above bitter partisanship and recognized the dangers to separation of powers if they abused their power of impeachment.

- The Johnson impeachment result confirmed the precedent of the Chase trial; policy disagreements and "harangues" do not meet the test for "high Crimes and Misdemeanors."

Judge Mark H. Delahay
Date of final Senate action: no action
Result: resigned

In 1872, the House passed a resolution authorizing a judiciary committee inquiry into Judge Mark H. Delahay, whose "personal habits unfitted him for the judicial office" given "that he was intoxicated off the bench as well as on the bench," according to "the most grievous charge." Procedurally, the House adopted its committee's proposed resolution of impeachment for "high Crimes and Misdemeanors in Office" in 1873, but Judge Delahay resigned before the articles of impeachment were prepared.[223]

KEY LESSON FROM THE DELAHAY CASE

- Congressional willingness and readiness to proceed with impeachment can achieve a beneficial result—resignation of a poorly performing officer—avoiding further substantial harm to the country. Resignation achieves the impeachment goal of removing malperforming officers.

Secretary of War William Belknap
Date of final Senate action: August 1, 1876
Result: not guilty, previously resigned

In 1876, President Ulysses S. Grant's secretary of war William Belknap appointed his friend Caleb P. Marsh to the lucrative position of post trader at Fort Sill, Oklahoma. Through Marsh or Marsh's intermediary, the secretary of war or his wife received large sums of money from his appointee.

Consistent with careful House practice, the House did not impeach on "Bribery" but rather on "High Crimes and Misdemeanors in Office." In five separate, detailed articles, overlapping in assertions, the House made clear that the secretary of war had received "large sums of money" in consideration for appointing Marsh; that the secretary of war had taken and received money for the continued maintenance of the trader in his post; and that his conduct was willful, unlawful, corrupt, and in criminal disregard of his duty.[224]

Belknap resigned shortly before impeachment articles were adopted in the House and thus before the trial in the Senate, which became a Senate trial fraught with confusion. Many senators, considering the effect of Belknap's earlier resignation, voted not guilty, and the Senate acquitted the already-resigned secretary of war. Twenty-two of the senators voting "not guilty" on each article indicated that, in their view, the Senate had no jurisdiction.[225]

KEY LESSONS FROM THE BELKNAP CASE

- As with the case of Senator Blount—an impeachment trial resulting in "Dismissal"—the Belknap Senate trial reinforced the need for Congress to craft better rules and more orderly processes for handling reactions—such as resignation—to impeachment, as well as better methods for conveying information and coordinating trial with the Senate. (Congress greatly improved over the years; streamlined processes in modern times brought about resignations when even the criminal justice system was helpless to remove from office a criminally convicted officer.)

- Congress may and will charge acts appearing to be well-orchestrated crimes such as bribery—and even use language in articles claiming criminal wrongdoing—but Congress does not charge the impeachable conduct as constitutional bribery; but rather characterizes the charges as a form of "other high Crimes and Misdemeanors."

Judge Charles Swayne
Date of final Senate action: February 27, 1905
Result: not guilty

Judge Robert Archbald
Date of final Senate action: January 13, 1913
Result: guilty, removed from office, disqualified from holding any office of honor, trust, or profit under the United States

Judge George W. English
Date of final Senate action: December 13, 1926
Result: resigned, charges dismissed

Judge Harold Louderback
Date of final Senate action: May 24, 1933
Result: not guilty

Judge Halsted Ritter
Date of final Senate action: April 17, 1936
Result: guilty, removed from office

In the first decades of the twentieth century, abuse of office for financial gain dominated the impeachment scene, with the impeachment of four federal judges, with additional serious tyranny and oppression charges against one judge (English) who combined massive financial misconduct with multiple deprivations of constitutional rights of the litigants, lawyers, jurors, criminal defendant, and public who learned—beyond the borders of his judicial district—of the absence of justice in his courtroom.

In 1903, Judge Charles Swayne was charged and impeached by the House for specific, alleged financial abuses: submitting false travel expense accounts, using a private railroad car without compensating the railroad company, living outside his judicial district in violation of the law, and misuse of his powers in imprisoning two lawyers for contempt.[226] Judge Swayne was impeached in 1903 and was acquitted in 1905.[227]

Judge Robert Archbald abused his office in many outrageous and significant ways for personal profit. He was impeached on thirteen articles and found guilty on five—including a "catch-all" article that summarized his misconduct as a federal district judge and federal commerce court judge, and his use of these offices "wrongfully to obtain credit," receiving hidden financial interests in diverse agreements—in the final Senate action of January 13, 1913.

The five articles under which Judge Archbald was convicted bear reading, not only for the breathtaking scope of financial improprieties, but also because the House wisely charged each and every one under "high Crimes and Misdemeanors," rather than a higher standard of a legal crime in the United States, requiring a higher level of intent. Here are the charges (1, 3, 4, 5, and 13) on which Judge Archbald was convicted:

The judge was charged with inducing companies who were litigants to effect a sale "so that he could make a profit"; using his position to obtain a corporation to lease, operate, and ship; engaging in secret communications with one side in a suit before him, in "gross and improper contacts" regarding a witness and his testimony; accepting a "gift, reward or present" for his attempts to secure for another an operating lease that had previously been refused; seeking credit from and through persons "who were interested in a result of suits then pending and suits that had been pending" in his court; settling lawsuits and speculating in properties; and receiving an interest in properties without investing any money or other thing of value in consideration.[228]

Judge Archbald was also impeached for misconduct prior to his then-current federal position on the Commerce Court—earlier wrongdoing that had occurred in a prior, impeachable federal judicial position as a district judge.[229] (A century later, Judge Porteous would be impeached for misconduct including lies and cover-up of corrupt relationships in his federal nomination process, with his corrupt relationships long predating his federal service.)[230] In addition to his conviction and removal, Judge Archbald was disqualified from holding any office of honor, trust, or profit under the United States.[231]

In 1926, Judge George English was impeached for a wide

variety of oppressive, tyrannical, and financial abuses, including misuse of his office for personal profit, colluding with a bankruptcy referee for profit, threatening to imprison newspapermen for public criticism, and creating a nonexistent case in order to verbally abuse state and local officials.

The House spread the charges against Judge English—taking care to plead substantial effect—into five articles, with Article 1 focusing on his abuse of the powers of his office amounting to tyranny and oppression as he unlawfully disbarred lawyers, used an "imaginary case" to profanely denounce state and local officials and threaten lawyers with jail if they failed to find a defendant guilty, generally abused his authority, and brought the administration of justice into disrepute; Articles 2 through 4 catalogued Judge English's corruption with a bankruptcy referee and a bank he owned and favored, which employed his son, spreading the facts of his corruption across three articles; Article 5 made clear allegations that Judge English's treatment of the media, members of the bar, and litigants violated fundamental concepts of liberty and property rights, that he had refused to allow trial by jury, that he violated his oath of office, that he excited fear and distrust, and that he inspired "widespread belief" beyond his judicial district that his cases were decided on factors other than the merits. Judge English resigned before the Senate began his trial; the proceedings were discontinued.[232]

Judge Harold Louderback was also charged with using his office for personal gain and was impeached and acquitted in 1932. Both Judges English and Louderback were also charged with setting bankruptcy fees for bankruptcy receivers for personal profit, for which federal judge Halsted Ritter was impeached and convicted in 1936.[233]

Judge Halsted Ritter's impeachment is best remembered for the successful strategy of the House managers. The House began its inquiry in 1933, with a subcommittee taking evidence in 1933 and 1934.[234] The charges against Judge Ritter included corruption, practicing law while serving as judge, and preparing and filing false income tax returns.[235] The House managers charging Judge Ritter strategically amended and combined their best allegations of misconduct into one final article that repeated earlier charges. Judge Ritter was impeached on seven grounds; he was convicted on April 17, 1936, on the last article, and acquitted on the first six.[236]

KEY LESSONS FROM THE SWAYNE, ARCHBALD, ENGLISH, LOUDERBACK, AND RITTER CASES

- Congress demonstrates clear willingness to impeach and convict an officer for abuse of office for personal, financial gain.

- Facts and pleadings matter, especially in demonstrating significant societal effects of the alleged misconduct, maladministration, or other "high Crimes and Misdemeanors." Compare the alleged misconduct of Judge Peck in misuse of contempt with allegations against Judge English; the pleading against Peck was very narrow and confined as to harm, and ultimately unsuccessful. The pleadings against English, on the other hand—which prompted his resignation—included "divers" occasions of Judge English's misconduct and widespread, harmful impact on society.

- Strategies—particularly "catch-all" or "omnibus" articles— matter. The much-revised, broad "catch-all" provision in the Ritter case succeeded where the narrower provisions failed. The House can combine charges, restating facts and rewording allegations from separate articles, in hopes of gaining two-thirds supports of the senators to convict on at least one individual article.[237]

President Richard Nixon
Date of final Senate action: no action
Result: resigned

In the century between Civil War Reconstruction under President Andrew Johnson and the next presidential impeachment activity, two World Wars, the Great Depression, foreign conflicts and crises, and the increasing pace of modern society tested congressional-presidential-judicial relations and brought greater power to the presidency. Threats of impeachment by members of the House against several presidents included resolutions against President Truman for his handling of the Korean conflict, his firing of General MacArthur, and his attempt to nationalize the steel mills following unsuccessful labor negotiations—but none of the resolutions led to impeachment.[238]

The increasing experience and sophistication of the twentieth-century House would be brought to bear in the first major presidential impeachment investigation in over a century, involving President Richard Milhous Nixon.

After his election in 1968, in an attempt to locate and punish sources who disclosed his secret Cambodian war, in an effort to prevent further disclosures, and in order to secure his reelection, Nixon began systematic spying and implemention of a variety of illegal techniques, including electronic surveillance, mail interceptions, and the creation of a special White House unit designed to stop information leaks, called "the Plumbers." Bad plans and acts ran amok, from misuse of the Internal Revenue Service in order to conduct "field audits of those who are our opponents" to proposals for burglaries and wired prostitutes hired for entrapment of enemies. G. Gordon Liddy, general counsel of the Committee to Re-Elect the President, or CREEP, proposed physical assault and kidnapping of anti-Nixon demonstrators.[239]

Nixon's successful 1972 reelection campaign enlisted "dirty tricks" and law-breaking organized and executed by CREEP, including bugging, burglaries, bags of cash to pay off wrong-doers, and continued lies to cover up the illegal activities. CREEP's security coordinator led a bungled break-in of the Democratic National Committee in the Watergate complex. According to federal district judge John Sirica assigned to the case, after the arrests at the Watergate Office Building, Nixon and his co-conspirators knew "that if the truth were revealed, they would lose their coveted power," so they repeatedly broke the law through 1972–1973 "to protect their offices."[240] CREEP's chairman, Nixon's former attorney general John Mitchell, lied in denying the burglars operated on behalf of CREEP.[241]

In spring 1973, a special Senate committee formed and began investigating Watergate. Soon thereafter, Special Prosecutor Archibald Cox began his investigation and eventually subpoenaed the Nixon White House's tape recordings, the existence of which came to light during congressional investigation. In October 1973, Nixon ordered the firing of the special prosecutor issuing the subpoenas. A grand jury named the president as an unindicted co-conspirator, tying the president to the cover-up of the Watergate burglary, in the opinion of federal judge Sirica. In July of 1974, the Supreme Court upheld Judge Sirica's order to produce the tapes.[242]

The president and his conspirators had lied about the tapes' contents, which revealed that Nixon tried to prevent the FBI from investigating the Watergate break-in. The transcripts provided by Nixon proved inaccurate and misleading.[243]

The president's and his co-conspirators' efforts to obstruct the investigation—including the president's order firing the special prosecutor who originally subpoenaed the tapes—did not deter the Office of Special Prosecutor or Congress. The Senate Watergate committee and its counsel conducted a detailed investigation, contributing vital evidence and televising hearings.[244] The House Judiciary Committee worked on a bipartisan basis and issued the key House Judiciary Committee report recommending impeachment.[245]

On August 9, 1974—within two weeks of the House committee's impeachment recommendation and before the House could vote on the proposed articles of impeachment—President Nixon resigned. Nonetheless, the Watergate prosecutors persisted with criminal charges against numerous Watergate defendants, even after then-president Gerald Ford pardoned their unindicted co-conspirator, now former-president Nixon. On February 21, 1975, Judge Sirica sentenced three of the president's top men—John Mitchell, H. R. Haldeman, and John Ehrlichman—to two and a half to eight years in prison. More sentences followed, the penalties declining with Judge Sirica's retirement and passage of time.[246]

Judge Sirica handled the case from the Watergate break-in to the showdown with the president over the tapes. In 1979, he reflected on the importance of the specific evidence so needed by Congress, but which the president withheld until the court system functioned as intended. Sirica praised the free press; the news reporters who wouldn't drop a story when they were under pressure to do so; the House and Senate committees; members of Congress and congressional staff, who put aside politics to do unpleasant jobs; and, in particular, the courts, which "set the record straight," noting the lessons of the Watergate crisis: "that our system is not invulnerable to the arrogance of power, to mis-deeds by power hungry individuals, and that we must always be on guard against selecting such people as our leaders."[247]

In his reflections, Judge Sirica expressed hope in the efforts, post-Watergate, to curb misuse of campaign funds; to "make our presidential elections more fair by preventing single, large contributors from having too great an influence on the outcome"; and in legislation "to force public officials (including judges) to disclose their financial assets and income, so the public can be reassured that those officials have not been bought and paid for by some special interest."[248]

The hard work of Congress praised by Judge Sirica and later by Chief Justice Rehnquist for its bipartisanship and thoughtfulness also produced the well-respected 1974 impeachment staff report of the House Judiciary Committee, "Constitutional Grounds for Presidential Impeachment."[249] The emerging impeachment grounds focusing on presidential abuse of power reflected the sophistication of the House managers, which by that point had been honed over almost two centuries.

The three articles of impeachment against President Nixon recommended by the House's committee—and used in the next presidential impeachment—provide a modern guide for charging presidential abuse of power, lying, cover up, violations of constitutional rights of U.S. citizens, and poaching by the executive on the powers of another branch of government.

Each article referenced the president's direct liability and liability for the wrongs of his agents and referenced broad, presidential duties and pleadings, showing a substantial scope of wrongful misconduct by the president—personally and through his agents. Duty violations included:

1. Acting "in a manner contrary to his trust as President and subversive of constitutional government, to the great prejudice of the cause of law and justice, and to the manifest injury of the people of the United States";
2. Violation of the president's duty to take care that the laws be faithfully executed;
3. Violation of the president's oath to faithfully execute the office and, to the best of his ability, preserve, protect, and defend the Constitution of the United States.

Article 1 charged that the president "has prevented, obstructed, and impeded the administration of justice," with additional language later charging misconduct of the president "using the powers of his high office, engaged personally through his subordinates and agents" in a course of conduct or plan designed to delay, impede, and obstruct investigation and to cover up, conceal, and protect those responsible for the existence and scope of other unlawful, covert activities.

Factually, Article 1 focused on the agents of the Committee to Re-Elect the President, specifically on their June 1972 burglary of the headquarters of the Democratic National Committee, to obtain political intelligence; Article 1 continued with eight detailed subcharges, including:

- Making false or misleading statements to investigating U.S. officers and employees, withholding evidence, witness tampering, interfering with investigations, paying secret substantial sums of money to buy silence and affect witnesses, misuse of the CIA, and leaking Department of Justice information to subjects of investigation to aid and assist them in avoiding criminal liability;

- Making false or misleading public statements for the purpose of deceiving the people of the United States into believing a thorough and complete investigation had been concluded with regard to investigative branch misconduct and CREEP personnel and that "there was no involvement" of the executive branch and campaign personnel in misconduct;

- Trying to cause prospective defendants to expect favors for their helpful, false testimony or silence; or rewarding persons for silence or false testimony.

Article 2 charged that the president repeatedly engaged in conduct violating constitutional rights of citizens and that he impaired due and proper administration of justice and conduct of lawful inquiries or contravening laws governing executive branch agencies and the purposes of those agencies.

Many of the same facts were used in Article 2 as Article 1, including the Watergate burglary and cover-up, but in a different context of gross abuses of constitutional rights, with five detailed subcharges against the president and his agents that included:

- Wrongful attempts to use the IRS against citizens' constitutional rights;

- Misuse of FBI, Secret Service, and other executive personnel in violation or disregard of citizens' constitutional rights;

- Maintenance of a secret investigational unit, financed in part from campaign contributions, using the CIA in covert and unlawful activities, and violation of constitutional rights of citizens, including attempts to prejudice the right of an accused to a fair trial;

- Knowledge, or reason to know, that his close subordinates were impeding investigation into illegal activity and cover-ups, including those related to the confirmation of Attorney General Richard Kleindienst, surveillance of citizens, the break-in at the office of Dr. Lewis Fielding (the psychiatrist of Daniel Ellsberg, who leaked the Pentagon Papers), and campaign financing practices of the Committee to Re-Elect the President; and

- "In disregard of the rule of law, [the knowing misuse of] the executive power by interfering with agencies of the executive branch" including the FBI, the Criminal Division, the Office of Watergate Special Prosecution Force, the Department of Justice, and the CIA, "in violation of his duty to take care that the laws be faithfully executed."

Article 3 charged the president with failure to produce "papers and things" pursuant to congressional subpoenas that sought material, relevant information, "assuming to himself functions and judgments as necessary to the exercise of the sole power of impeachment vested by the Constitution in the House of Representatives."

Factually, Article 3 laid out the dates of the subpoenas and the president's noncompliance. The president failed to produce papers and things, as directed, without lawful cause, pursuant to duly authorized subpoenas from the House Committee on the Judiciary, substituting his judgment as to what materials were necessary, and thus "interposed the powers of the Presidency against the lawful subpoenas of the House."[250]

Two other articles were not voted out of committee.[251]

KEY LESSONS FROM THE RICHARD NIXON CASE

- The very existence of the ongoing impeachment process worked quickly to protect the country from harm. The House Judiciary Committee propelled President Nixon toward impeachment when they voted to send articles to impeach to the House of Representatives. The readiness of the House and Senate to proceed with impeachment caused the president to remove himself from office. The 1974 House staff report, providing a history of U.S. impeachment to that point in time, taught that impeachment was intended to reach a broad variety of conduct, including breach of duty; "the American impeachment cases demonstrate a common theme useful in determining whether grounds of impeachment exist—that the grounds are derived from understanding the nature, functions and duties of the office."[252]

The 1974 staff report provided clear legal guidance, used in the subsequent Clinton case, particularly in terms of drafting the charges and understanding the limits of impeachment where the House cannot prove the scope of harmful effect. The legal conclusions of the 1974 report are repeatedly cited in modern impeachments:

1. A requirement of criminality would be incompatible with the framers' intention to provide a mechanism broad enough to maintain the integrity of constitutional government;
2. Impeachment is a constitutional safety valve, and to fulfill this function, it must be flexible enough to cope with exigencies not now foreseeable;
3. The emphasis of American impeachment practices has been on the "significant effects of the conduct—undermining the integrity of the office, disregard of constitutional duties and oath of office, arrogation of power, abuse of the governmental process, adverse impact on the system of government."[253]

The careful work of the House left a record of what some of the best minds at the time concluded were grounds for presidential impeachment, including cover-up and obstruction, responsibility for cover-ups by subordinates, misleading or deceiving the public, misuse of power, and violation of the oath of office. The emphasis on abuse of office, overreaching of presidential power, and violations of duties—and not on criminal charges—provided guidance for every judicial and presidential impeachment that followed.[254] The guidance included the following legal concepts:

1. The president is responsible for the wrongdoings of his agents and subordinates. The Nixon impeachment language included classic legal concepts of a principal responsible for his agents; the House recommended articles

of impeachment using language charging the president with using the powers of his high office, engaging personally "through his subordinates and agents" in a course of conduct or plan designed to delay, impede, and obstruct investigation, to cover up, conceal, and protect those responsible and to conceal the existence and scope of other unlawful, covert activities;

2. Even absent actual knowledge of wrongdoing, the president can be responsible if he "has reason to know." The recommended House articles charged that the president knew or had reason to know that his close subordinates were impeding investigation into illegal activity and cover-ups of such matters as surveillance of citizens, the break-in of the office of Daniel Ellsberg's psychiatrist, and illegal campaign financing practices of the Committee to Re-Elect the President;

3. Presidential misleading or lying to the public is actionable in impeachment. Congress, in Article 1 of the Nixon impeachment articles developed a template for charging the president with impeachable lying, using words such as "deceiving the public" and "making false or misleading public statements for the purpose of deceiving the people of the United States" in combination with factual allegations regarding the effect of the lies;

4. Fundamental violations of constitutional principles—particularly poaching on the sole powers of another branch of government—create substantial impeachment liability. An excellent example of poaching by a president on congressional power: interfering with investigations of the executive branch that might provide information relevant to congressional "sole" powers of impeachment. Independent of lying, presidential withholding of information is actionable in impeachment. Charges of violating separation of powers—and "sole" power of Congress in impeachment—works beautifully. Congress appropriately

emphasized that President Nixon stepped on the powers of other branches of government. President Nixon's attempts to avoid production of evidence, substituting his judgment as to what materials were necessary "interposed the powers of the Presidency against the lawful subpoenas of the House." He violated the basic, constitutional principle of separation of powers, "assuming to himself functions and judgments as necessary to the exercise of the sole power of impeachment vested by the Constitution in the House of Representatives."[255]

Sam Dash, the chief counsel of the Senate Watergate committee, reflected on the concept of separation of powers as he explained that the growth of executive power in the decades leading to Watergate and the emergence of "a President who believed he had absolute, unreviewable power,"[256] produced Watergate. Dash warned that history would repeat itself if we fail to heed its lessons, as he cited the depth of knowledge of the Constitution's framers in their construction of our system of government: "A free republic can best be preserved through checks and balances applied through the separation of governmental powers . . . The essential force to make it work is an alert, informed and active citizenry. That force, and consequently, a responsible, accountable government, were absent for at least half a century." Chief Counsel Dash, citing the first three words of the Constitution, recognized that "momentarily"—referencing only the time of Watergate—"we the people asserted ourselves and witnessed the remarkable impact on representative government. We turn away again at our own peril."[257]

Disregarding our cherished "rule of law" is actionable in impeachment as is violation of presidential duties to "take care" that the laws be faithfully executed. The Nixon case made famous the allegation of presidential misuse of power, and caused America to focus on the "rule of law" in the United

States as opposed to the "rule of man" we abhor in dictator-ships. Thus, the House Judiciary Committee charged that President Nixon, in "disregard of the rule of law ... knowingly misused the executive power by interfering with agencies of the executive branch" including the FBI, the Criminal Divi-sion, the Office of the Watergate Special Prosecution Force, the Department of Justice, and the CIA, "in violation of his duty to take care that the laws be faithfully executed."

Judge Harry E. Claiborne
Date of final Senate action: October 9, 1986
Result: guilty, removed from office

Judge Harry Claiborne was impeached by the House for pro-viding false information on federal income tax forms, the same facts which formed the basis of his earlier 1984 criminal convic-tion. The House charged and proved to the Senate under Ar-ticles 1 and 2 that the Judge engaged in misbehavior and high crimes and misdemeanors warranting removal. The Senate also convicted the judge on Article 4, which stated that the judge's actions brought the "judiciary into disrepute, thereby under-mining public confidence in the integrity and impartiality of the administration of justice." Found guilty on Articles 1, 2, and 4, Judge Claiborne was removed from office on October 9, 1986.[258]

The Senate did not, however, convict on Article 3, which claimed that the fact of a criminal conviction (in Judge Clai-borne's case, tax fraud) was the equivalent of a high crime in office. The Senate set thoughtful precedent in that Claiborne's "undermining public confidence in the integrity and impar-tiality of the administration of justice" can be impeachable with the right facts, but the mere commission of a crime is not in and of itself impeachable, without analysis of the underlying facts.[259]

The Claiborne trial also provided the Senate an excellent

opportunity to try out streamlined rules, which paved the way for more efficient trials. The Senate established a special trial committee to hear evidence and report to the full Senate, and Senate trial committees considered evidence in the later cases of Alcee Hastings (1989), Walter Nixon, Jr. (1989), and G. Thomas Porteous, Jr. (2010), all of whom were convicted and removed from office.[260]

KEY LESSONS FROM THE CLAIBORNE CASE

- The Claiborne case created important precedent—on personal misconduct giving rise to impeachment—for all future impeachment cases, including presidential impeachment.

- The Senate again proved that impeachment is in no way a criminal proceeding; thus, the Senate took on the burden to determine if underlying misconduct is an impeachable offense as distinguished from a crime. The Senate, sitting as a court of impeachment, required independent proof of impeachable misconduct, not the mere fact of prior criminal conviction. Such thoughtfulness leads to factual development and proof of the substantial harm and threat to society caused by the alleged "high Crimes and Misdemeanors."

- Congressionally streamlined procedures ensured future cases could run efficiently and well. Future impeachment defendants could not depend on a hope that Congress would bungle or be hamstrung by cumbersome proce- dures. These streamlined procedures served as a prompt for resignations from officials who knew their conduct would be scrutinized in future impeachment activity.[261]

Judge Alcee Hastings
Date of final Senate action: October 20, 1989
Result: guilty, removed from office

Judge Alcee Hastings, accused in criminal court of soliciting a bribe and acquitted in criminal proceedings, was later separately impeached and convicted of "impeachable offenses," which included lying and submitting false evidence in the criminal trial where he had been previously acquitted. In other words, Hastings lied in criminal court, which led to his acquittal. The House managers, with painstaking investigation, then exposed the lies that led to the criminal acquittal and also proved the Judge's underlying misconduct, charged as corruption. The House impeached and the Senate convicted, removing him from office on October 20, 1989.

Judge Hastings' impeachment is notable as the first time an official was impeached and tried after being acquitted in criminal court.[262] The House also impeached Judge Hastings for divulging confidential information from a wiretap, but there was no conviction on this allegation—which was included twice, once in a specific Article 16, and the second time in an aggregated, or omnibus, Article 17, which was a "catch-all" category.

Modern times have brought wiretap-violation impeachment activity. Also in 1989, federal judge Robert P. Aquilar was indicted for unlawful wiretap disclosure, leading to a House resolution to impeach. After seven years of criminal litigation, Judge Aquilar resigned from office, and no further action was taken on the House resolution to impeach.[263]

The Hastings impeachment articles allege "impeachable offense" without resorting to specific, constitutional language in the articles. Each of the seventeen articles, including the broad "catch-all," end as follows: "Wherefore, Judge Alcee L. Hastings is guilty of an impeachable offense warranting removal from office."[264]

KEY LESSONS FROM THE HASTINGS CASE

- The House managers may charge impeachment with the most flexible, basic language of "impeachable offenses."

- Hastings proves that impeachments are not criminal proceedings. Hastings was the first impeachment for misconduct after a criminal acquittal. The Senate's care in not relying on a criminal court conviction in Claiborne was vindicated in Hastings.

- As with Claiborne, the Hastings case was cited as precedent in future impeachments, setting standards for presidential as well as judicial impeachments.

Judge Walter Nixon
Date of final Senate action: November 3, 1989
Result: guilty, removed from office

Within a month of the Senate impeachment conviction of Judge Hastings, the Senate tried and convicted Walter L. Nixon, Jr., the former chief judge for the Southern District of Mississippi. Judge Nixon had accepted money from a Mississippi "businessman" in exchange for pleading for leniency for the businessman's son from a district attorney, then lied to the grand jury and investigators about the matter.

The House managers carefully charged Judge Nixon with "an impeachable offense" and the Senate process proceeded efficiently, holding four days of hearings during which the judge and nine other witnesses testified. The report and transcript were delivered to the entire Senate, which received extensive briefing and arguments and whose members posed questions.[265] On November 3, 1989, the Senate convicted on the two fact-rich articles, but did not convict on the third article, which repeated the facts and added general allegations of undermining confidence, of bringing disrepute to the federal judiciary, and of betrayal of trust.

Judge Nixon appealed his Senate impeachment conviction and removal, arguing that the Senate process of using a committee to hear evidence and report wasn't acceptable. Judge Nixon lost.[266]

In *Nixon v. United States*, Supreme Court Chief Justice Rehnquist made clear that the Senate indeed had sole power to try all cases of impeachment. The Supreme Court stated that "sole" means "sole," including "only one" and "functioning . . . independently and without assistance or interference."[267]

Speaking for the majority of the Court, Justice Rehnquist also offered practical, reasons of governance why the Supreme Court would not open the door of judicial review:

> [O]pening the door of judicial review to the procedures used by the Senate in trying impeachments would "expose the political life of the country to months, or perhaps years, of chaos . . .

> The legitimacy of any successor, and hence his effectiveness would be impaired seriously, not merely while the judicial process was running its course, but during any retrial that a differently constituted Senate might conduct if its first judgment of conviction were invalidated. Equally uncertain is the question of what relief a court may give other than simply setting aside the judgment of conviction.[268]

KEY LESSONS FROM THE WALTER NIXON CASE

- The Judge Nixon impeachment case demonstrates again that streamlined, efficient procedures minimize the chance for massive communication errors in the future, providing a deterrent to wrongdoers who, in earlier days, might have hoped Congress would not act.

- The House will charge financial misconduct and abuse of office for personal gain—including the acceptance of bribes—as either "high Crimes and Misdemeanors" or as "impeachable offenses," and not as constitutional bribery.

- The Supreme Court decision in *Nixon v. United States* stands solidly for the proposition that the Senate has the final authority to determine how it will "try" impeached officers under the Impeachment Clause.[269]

President William J. Clinton
Date of final Senate action: February 12, 1999
Result: not guilty

The impeachment of President Clinton began as an investigation by independent counsel regarding alleged financial improprieties—supposed pressure for a favorable loan—when President Clinton was Arkansas governor. When the original counsel was replaced in August 1994, the investigation morphed and grew over five years to allege improprieties in the White House travel office and alleged misuse of personnel files, on which no impeachment articles came and upon which the president was "eventually exonerated."[270] The independent counsel expanded his inquiry to investigate an alleged sexual relationship between the president and White House intern Monica Lewinsky and alleged aid the president gave the intern in finding other employment, as well as Paula Jones's claims—in 1994 civil litigation—of sexual harassment in 1991 by then-governor Bill Clinton. In January 1998, the president gave a deposition in the Jones civil lawsuit, where he was questioned about Lewin-

sky and denied a sexual relationship, stating that the intern's affidavit statements denying the sexual relationship were true.[271]

A federal grand jury, impaneled by the special prosecutor,
heard much evidence, including Lewinsky's August 6 and August 20, 1998, testimony of her sexual relationship with the
president, which she said began in November 1995, when she
was twenty-two.[272] She testified that she was not asked to lie
about the relationship.[273] The president testified to the grand
jury from the White House on August 17, 1998, acknowledging
"inappropriate intimate" contact, in his opening statement,[274]
but parsing words as to whether his conduct, which involved
oral sex, constituted sexual relations.[275]

After his grand jury testimony, the president publicly admitted he had misled people, but still insisted his testimony had
been "legally accurate," and that he never asked anyone to lie,
hide, destroy evidence, or act unlawfully.[276]

In September 1998, the Office of Independent Counsel delivered to the House a report on its investigation and identified
eleven grounds for impeachment. The report focused on allegations that included the following: perjury in the deposition
and grand jury as well as obstruction of justice in concealing
his relationship with Lewinsky and helping her find a job in
New York, exchange of gifts, and claims the president had an
understanding with Lewinsky to hide their affair. The report
concluded the president abused his constitutional authority by
lying, repeatedly, to hinder possible inquiry by Congress.[277]

The Judiciary Committee of the House and its subcommittee
on the Constitution entertained many submissions and much
testimony on the meaning of high crimes and misdemeanors,
and whether President Clinton's misconduct qualified as such,
whether the concept of a president being unfit for office was too
amorphous a criterion for impeachment, and whether some
transgressions were best left to the electorate.[278] After debate on
the articles of impeachment on December 18 and 19, 1998, the
House voted generally along party lines to adopt two articles

focusing on President Clinton's attempts to cover up his affair: the first article, centering on lying—perjury—and the third article, involving concealment and obstruction of justice.[279]

The claimed violations of duty subjecting the president to impeachment, per the two Clinton articles of impeachment (renumbered below) that were sent to the Senate, repeated the three broad constitutional duties identified by the 1974 staff report and used in the recommended articles against President Nixon, stating that the president:

1. Violated the president's constitutional oath to faithfully execute the office;
2. Violated the president's constitutional oath promising to the best of his ability to preserve, protect, and defend the Constitution of the United States; and
3. Violated the president's constitutional duty to take care that the law be faithfully executed.

Both Articles 1 and 2 contained common claims that President Clinton undermined the integrity of the office, brought disrepute on the presidency, betrayed his trust as president, and acted in manner subversive of the rule of law and justice, to manifest injury to people of the United States.

Article 1 charged that President Clinton:

• Willfully corrupted and manipulated the judicial process of the United States for his personal gain and exoneration, impeding the administration of justice;

• Provided perjurious false, misleading testimony to the grand jury on August 17, 1998, regarding his relations with a "subordinate Government employee," false testimony in the federal civil rights case filed by Paula Jones, and allowed false statements by his attorney in that litigation, and made corrupt efforts to influence testimony and impede discovery.

Article 2 (formerly Article 3 in the House proposal) charged that President Clinton:

- In overview, prevented, obstructed, and impeded the administration of justice; acted personally, and through his subordinates and agents, engaged in a course of conduct or scheme designed to delay, impede, cover up and conceal the existence of evidence and testimony related to the federal civil rights action brought against him.

The factual allegations provided dates between December 17, 1997, and January 26, 1998, when the president was alleged to have encouraged a witness to swear to a false affidavit; encouraged a witness to give false, perjurious, or misleading testimony if called; concealed evidence; secured job assistance to a witness against him to corruptly prevent truthful testimony; corruptly allowed his attorney to make a false statement, subsequently acknowledged; on at least three dates, related a false and misleading account; made false and misleading statements in order to corruptly influence testimony; and on three dates made false and misleading statements which were repeated by grand jury witnesses, causing the grand jury to receive false information.[280]

On February 12, 1999, the Senate voted to acquit President Clinton in votes on both articles of impeachment.

Even by the losing prosecution's account, the process had worked. House impeachment manager Lindsey Graham concluded: "The president has been cleansed . . . The cloud from the White House, constitutionally, has been blown away."[281]

KEY LESSONS FROM THE CLINTON CASE

- Judicial impeachment cases are solid precedent in presidential impeachment. Congress made full use of judicial impeachment cases as precedent in the Clinton impeach-

ment and Senate trial, using the cases of Judges Claiborne
(who falsified tax returns) and Walter Nixon (who lied to a
grand jury and investigators) in focusing on impeachability
of a president for claims involving personal misconduct,
unrelated to official duties. The Clinton case stands for the
proposition that, with presidents as with judges, there is
one impeachment standard and it is "high Crimes and Misdemeanors," a flexible standard, as emphasized by the 1974
staff report and the standard by which every U.S. impeachment case has been decided. The importance of judicial
impeachment precedent in presidential impeachment
cannot be overstated. Judicial impeachments—the only
impeachment convictions in U.S. history to date—provide
thoughtful guidance in a variety of areas which follow.

- A judicial or executive branch official—including the
  president—can be impeached regardless of whether his
  conduct was "an abuse of official power."[282] The Clinton case cements the proposition already understood
  in judicial case—a proposition Congress argued force-
  fully—that a president's personal misconduct, outside
  the scope of power or duties, is impeachable. The House
  Judiciary Committee report that recommended articles
  of impeachment argued that perjury by the president was
  an impeachable offense, even if committed with regard to
  matters outside his official duties, rejecting the idea that
  conduct such as perjury was more detrimental when committed by judges and therefore only impeachable when
  committed by judges.[283] The House Clinton report language pointed to Judge Claiborne, whose falsification of
  income tax returns was an act that "betrayed the trust of
  the people of the United States and reduced confidence in
  the integrity and impartiality of the judiciary." While it is
  "devastating" for the judiciary when judges are perceived

as dishonest, the report argued, perjury by the president was "just as devastating to our system of government." In addition, the report continued, both Judge Claiborne and Judge Nixon were impeached and convicted for perjury and false statements in matters distinct from their official duties. Likewise, the report noted the president's perjurious conduct, though seemingly falling outside of his official duties, nonetheless constituted grounds for impeachment.[284]

- The term "high Crimes and Misdemeanors" is not limited to "large scale abuses of public office—similar to treason and bribery."[285] Some advocates for the Minority in the Clinton impeachment urged that presidential impeachment be limited not only to official executive abuses of power, but to misconduct on par with "Treason" or "Bribery," the two bad acts listed in the Constitution, to which George Mason added "other high Crimes and Misdemeanors." This Minority argument ignores the framers' statements that incapacity or negligence, for example, with sufficient injury to society, warrants impeachment. The Senate—in acquitting President Clinton, despite serious claims of perjury and obstruction (intentional acts)—understood the lessons of the 1974 staff report and the Founding Fathers that Congress should look to the effect, the harm to society, the "substantiality" of the abuse, not whether the conduct or abuse was on par with treason.[286]

- Pleading substantial harm does not amount to proof of substantial harm. The prosecution focused on President Clinton's roles in government, including serving as head of the Department of Justice, but could not provide sufficient proof on the most important element: impeachment requires "substantiality" in maladministration, that which is seriously incompatible with the constitutional form and principles of our government or the proper performance of constitutional duties of the office.[287] Substantial effect, which was pled only generally,[288] was not proved.

- President Clinton's case also formalized the impeachment liability of a president for his various duties. Congress heard testimony and discussed the breadth of responsibilities under the presidential oath of office and the "Take Care Clause" that the laws be faithfully executed, discussed the judicial impeachment cases, and confirmed the impeachability of financial misconduct and lying, where misconduct calls into question integrity, truthfulness, and fitness.[289] The scope of presidential liability is defined by the scope of his roles, uniquely greater in scope than those of any other U.S. officer. The Clinton-impeachment House managers' emphasis of the role of president as head of the Department of Justice, in focusing on his liability for lying, built on the Nixon impeachment articles.

- The modern House regards its role as "to accuse"—as did Alexander Hamilton[290]—leaving the Senate with the great responsibility either to acquit or convict. House Republicans analogized their role to a grand jury, to determine whether there was sufficient evidence to "indict."[291] Congresswoman Elizabeth Holtzman urged the committee not to vote for impeachment "unless there is a strong likelihood of conviction in the Senate,"[293] but the House clearly disagreed.

- In the Clinton impeachment, the House and the Senate built on centuries of experience and rules. Using strategies based on the Nixon investigation, Congress placed duties on the defense to respond to inquiries, thereby creating new issues of "obstruction of justice," with regard to investigative obligations during the impeachment process. The speed with which Congress can move, or change deadlines, allows it to continue momentum, while the process remains politicized;[295] the prosecutors in the Clinton impeachment case, dissatisfied with what they characterized as technical answers and legalistic defenses, used the answers in claiming further obstruction of justice,[294] with rejected Article 4 focusing on abuse of office.

- The Clinton impeachment trial built on the efficiencies learned and used under new rules in the Claiborne impeachment. The Clinton trial offers examples of modern techniques and flexibility, including fact presentations, interim vote on whether to dismiss, limited witnesses, and use of video depositions.[295]

- The Clinton case reinforces the basic impeachment concept that not every crime is impeachable. Indeed, the Clinton acquittal proves that the crime (perjury) many people believed to have been proved was so insubstantial in effect on the country that impeachment was unwarranted.

Judge Samuel B. Kent
Date of final Senate action: July 22, 2009
Result: resigned, case dismissed

Samuel B. Kent was a federal judge for two decades. He was the sole federal judge on Galveston Island on the Texas Gulf Coast for the Southern District of Texas for nearly his entire career—from his appointment by President George H. W. Bush in 1990 until 2008. Kent proudly self-identified as a tyrant, "the Government," and "the Emperor of Galveston," wielding federal power, and, for years—as he finally confessed—sexually assaulting his employees.[296]

Kent used his power to intimidate women with uncontested boasts of power and continued threats to take away victims' jobs in order to force federal courthouse employees into sexual acts and to cover up his misconduct. Kent told a victim that he would not tolerate disloyalty or "talking out of school," and that he was the sole person responsible for his personal staff's hiring and firing. "He also told me that he was the Government—'I am the Government'; 'I'm the Lion King—it's good to be king'; 'I'm the Emperor of Galveston'; and 'the man wearing the horned hat, guiding the ship.'" [297]

The first victim to report Judge Kent's assaults was a deputy clerk who was assigned to Judge Kent's courtroom. The clerk reported her complaint to the Fifth Circuit Court of Appeals in May 2007, and, two weeks later, Judge Kent—at his own request—met with investigators and lied. A second victim eventually came forward and testified to years of sexual and psychological abuse from the federal judge, which began on her fifth day of work. She described his lying and manipulation, including his lying statements in the newspaper.[298] One of the victims disclosed terror-filled attacks with security guards nearby, despite her reports to fearful managers who did nothing. While the victim begged the judge to stop, she said Kent told her:

> . . . [h]e didn't care because he knew everyone was afraid of him. I later found out how true that was. He had the power to end careers and affect everyone's livelihood. That incident left me emotionally wrecked and humiliated. It was so difficult to face my coworkers when I knew they had seen what happened to me . . .

> The last assault I had was more terrifying and threatening than ever before. After forcing himself upon me and asking me to do unspeakable things, he told me that pleasuring him was something I owed him. That was

it for me. He had finally won. He had broken me and forced me out. I could handle no more of his abuse.

Keep in mind that I had already reported his behavior to my manager. She knew about the assaults from the very beginning . . . she was also very afraid of him. She had experienced his inappropriate behavior herself . . .

Every employee in Galveston has been afraid of his power and control.[299]

After the report to federal authorities, Kent continued to lie and intimidate witnesses, telling a victim that he had denied her allegations and she must also lie.[300] The chief judge of the Fifth Circuit suspended Judge Kent and transferred him to Houston.[301]

The Department of Justice pursued a criminal investigation. Kent lied to the Fifth Circuit, to the FBI, and to the Department of Justice, including telling bold lies to the chief of the Public Integrity Unit and the acting assistant attorney general. The grand jury indicted on three counts, including abusive sexual conduct, specific acts of forced sexual contact, aggravated sexual abuse, and obstruction of justice by Judge Kent.[302]

On February 23, 2009, Kent finally admitted to lying and to the nonconsensual sexual conduct, pleading guilty to obstruction of justice.

On May 11, 2009, following his February 23, 2009 guilty plea, Judge Kent was sentenced to thirty-three months of incarceration, payment of a fine, and ordered to pay restitution to his victims. He was required to surrender to prison no later than June 15, 2009.[303] Kent's victims testified at the sentencing hearing, captured in the House report submitted by Congressman John Conyers, from the committee on the judiciary.[304]

Kent, shortly to enter prison, spent his time scheming to preserve the great benefits and lifetime salary of a federal judge.

The fifty-nine-year-old judge had tried—and been thwarted by the Fifth Circuit—to retire early and retain his benefits. He sought a disability-based retirement to provide him a lifetime salary, and was again thwarted by the Fifth Circuit. Then, in early June, 2009, Kent offered a non-binding "resignation," to supposedly take place a year in the future—unless he withdrew it—allowing him to remain a federal judge in prison, and as such continue to draw his $174,000 annual salary and benefits. The resignation letter was regarded as a ploy, as the *Houston Chronicle* reported:

> Although Kent announced . . . his intention to resign June 1, 2010, the only way to remove Kent and end his $174,000 salary is by impeachment in the House and conviction in the Senate. U.S. Rep. Bob Goodlatte, R-Va, said Kent's resignation letter isn't worth the paper it is written on. "There is nothing to prevent him withdrawing his resignation any time," Goodlatte said.[305]

Congress stood ready to act with regard to Judge Kent. Soon after Judge Kent's sentencing, the House passed a resolution establishing an impeachment task force.[306] Congress acted in a bipartisan, intelligent, thorough, and forceful manner, independent of the criminal actions bringing Kent to prison.

Congress moved forward with impeachment proceedings. The House task force held an evidentiary hearing on June 3, 2009, which included testimony from both the victims and an expert witness.[307] Judge Kent and his lawyer declined to appear at the hearing.[308] Both victims again provided dramatic testimony explaining the assaults the judge had committed and the clear objections they had made to try to stop him. The second witness provided much testimony on Judge Kent's view of power, and his warnings that "talking out of school" would result in her and any staff members' "immediate dismissal."[309] This witness, threatened by Judge Kent, didn't tell her complete story until her third appearance in front of the grand jury.[310]

On June 19, 2009, the House impeached Kent for "high Crimes and Misdemeanors," on four separate articles, each adopted with no opposition,[311] which charged him with massive lies and repeated, nonconsensual sexual assaults of his employees.[312]

Kent's lawyer restated to the *Houston Chronicle* his opinion that the Senate would not convict. Senate majority leader Harry Reid, through a spokesman, told the *Chronicle* that the Senate was hoping to make the trial "as timely as possible." Kent waited until he was served with a congressional summons in prison to finally hand over a "no frills" resignation.[313]

KEY LESSONS FROM THE KENT CASE

- The House and Senate, performing their work efficiently, have a powerful, effective influence on badly performing officials. Two powerful forces caused Judge Sam Kent to resign: (1) the thorough, orderly action of the House, with no opposition, and (2) the Senate's stated willingness to proceed to trial, with procedures within their sole constitutional authority, per the Supreme Court decision in *Nixon v. United States.*[314]

- Impeachment works as an embedded part of our democracy. The Senate, with a simple, public statement from its leader, finished off a tyrant.[315]

- Impeachment is a noncriminal proceeding. The House report emphasized that, while the Kent case involved criminal misconduct, impeachment carries no such requirement. In "A Brief Discussion of Impeachment,"[316] its report to accompany the House resolution concerning the impeachment of Judge Kent, the House cited the House reports accompanying the resolutions to impeach Judges Nixon and Hastings concerning the meaning of "high Crimes and Misdemeanors," noting that impeachment is "non criminal" and serves "simply to remove the offender from office" and that impeachment is "the ultimate means of preserving our constitutional form of government from the depredations of those who abuse or violate the public trust."[317]

G. Thomas Porteous, Jr.
Date of final Senate action: December 8, 2010
Result: guilty, removed from office, barred from future federal office holding

Federal judge G. Thomas Porteous, Jr., failed to disclose his part in a long-standing corrupt scheme (beginning in the 1980s, when the judge was on a state court) with two lawyers in a firm, refused to recuse himself from a case where a party was represented by that very same law firm with whom he had the corrupt relationships, "solicited and accepted things of value" (as the articles of impeachment broadly charged)[318] from a bail bondsman and his sister in return for years of favors from the bench, and ruled in favor of the attorneys who'd paid him. In 1994, when nominated to the federal bench, he lied on his federal disclosure forms and background check, to the FBI and to the Senate. And, knowing the bail bondsman had also lied to the FBI about the corrupt relationships with the law firm and him, Judge Porteous failed to disclose the corrupt relationships or disclose he knew that the persons were lying in order to assure Porteous's appointment.

The impeachment investigation of Judge Porteous began in 2008. He was impeached on March 11, 2010, and he was convicted on December 8, 2010, on each of four articles of impeachment alleging "high Crimes and Misdemeanors": corrupt financial relationships, corrupt schemes and patterns of activity, many lies, and his knowledge that his fellow schemers were also lying to cover for him prior to his elevation to the federal bench.[319]

He was therefore removed from office and—in a rare decision—the Senate then voted 94 to 2 to disqualify Judge Porteous from holding any future federal office. Porteous therefore joined Judges Humphreys and Archbald, both convicted in impeachment (and therefore removed from office) and then disqualified by separate Senate vote from holding any future federal office.[320]

Article 4, a separate ground for conviction, dealt with Judge Porteous's wrongdoing before he took the federal bench: lies and cover-up during the nomination process. The charge included Judge Porteous's wrongdoing, which "deprived the United States Senate and the public of information that would have had a material impact on his confirmation."

KEY LESSONS FROM THE PORTEOUS CASE

- Judge Porteous is the first impeached, convicted U.S. officer for whom prior misconduct as a nominee for a federal position gave rise to independent impeachment liability and conviction during the federal nomination process. (Judge Archbald's misconduct in prior positions occurred in other federal, impeachable positions.) Judge Porteous's long-standing corrupt relationships with crooked colleagues also pre-dated his federal nomination and federal position, but the impeachment allegations of pre-federal (and pre-federal-nominee) misconduct are mixed with federal misconduct; therefore, we do not know whether his state court, pre-nomination conduct served as independent basis for impeachment. Article 4, however, independently focused on misconduct during his nomination process; the judge's lies, cover-up, and other misconduct as federal nominee gave rise to independent impeachment liability.[321]

- Combined with the case of Judge Kent, in 2009, the Porteous case demonstrates the virtues of improved processes and availability of impeachment as an efficient device to remove malfunctioning public officials.

- The House charged and the Senate convicted on serious bribery and corruption matters as "high Crimes and Misdemeanors" instead of charging under constitutional bribery or bribery statutes. Personal misconduct—bankruptcy fraud under Article 3—proved actionable in impeachment. Thus, "high Crimes and Misdemeanors" remains the accepted, appropriate mechanism for charging what the Senate believes are very serious risks to society.[322]

CONCLUSION

Researching and writing this book was a learning experience beyond measure. Studying this history gives me great confidence in the genius of our Founding Fathers, and it is comforting to know the degree to which political figures across the spectrum of time and party loyalties honor the constitutional impeachment process, from the Founding Fathers in the eighteenth century advocating its use as the proper constitutional alternative to "tumults and insurrection" to its effective use against modern tyrants and self-styled emperors.

Thus, this book naturally cites public officials and scholars across the centuries and political spectrum including Supreme Court Justice William Brennan and the Heritage Foundation for their teachings on the pardon power; Pulitzer Prize–winning author, Democrat, and then–future president John F. Kennedy on the key points of the impeachment of Andrew Johnson; and then–Republican House manager Lindsey Graham, who went on to become a Republican senator and contributed greatly to modernizing impeachment law by understanding and using cases of judicial impeachment as appropriate precedent in the impeachment of President Bill Clinton. In the impeachment of Judge Sam Kent, Congressman John Conyers—a Democrat—submitted a key House of Representatives report, while Senator Harry Reid—the Democratic Senate leader—spoke the reassuring words of Senate willingness to proceed to impeachment trial, causing the resignation of abusive Judge Kent, serving his prison sentence for obstruction of justice. One outstanding educational source in the use of impeachment proved to be Republican presidential appointee to the Supreme Court Chief Justice William Rehnquist, who presided over the Clinton impeachment trial.

We should appreciate the role of Chief Justice Rehnquist in our country's twenty-first-century use of impeachment. At the end of the twentieth century and into the twenty-first, Congress has undertaken multiple impeachment investigations and increasingly used its impeachment powers. Congressional work, the subject of public praise—unusually—by the then–sitting Chief Justice William Rehnquist of the U.S. Supreme Court in his 1992 impeachment book, *Grand Inquests*, demonstrates the strength of our democracy in general and our impeachment practices in particular.[323] The chief justice made it very clear that future generations had "considerable room" to adapt impeachment for future contingencies the Founding Fathers could not anticipate; they left us "play in the joints" to use the Impeachment Clause for the good of the country.[324] Justice Rehnquist's 1993 Supreme Court opinion in *Nixon v. United States* cemented the Senate's power to choose its own impeachment procedures, bringing finality and certainty to the impeachment verdicts of the U.S. Senate, reiterating Alexander Hamilton's faith in its deliberative powers.

The United States uses one standard for both judicial and executive impeachments. The massive 1970s Richard Nixon House investigation and related research, which produced the 1974 staff report, followed by the late 1980s Clinton impeachment materials implementing many of those concepts, make clear (for anyone who doubted) that the standard for judicial impeachment and presidential impeachment are one and the same: "other high Crimes and Misdemeanors."

A Congress experienced and prepared to efficiently impeach and try cases, well educated and well prepared on the nature of duties and harm involved, and with an understanding of the flexible scope of "high Crimes and Misdemeanors," can confidently, with precedent, deter some misconduct, cause resignations, and—when necessary—remove malfunctioning officers who pose substantial risk to the country we love. The Impeachment Clause in the twenty-first century has reached stability and maturity with increasing use, experience, and precedent. The Impeachment Clause remains as necessary, exciting, and important as when Madison, Morris, and Mason debated it, when Alexander Hamilton predicted it would check executive abuse of power, and when James Madison explained its necessity to protect against a president's betrayal of trust to a foreign power, negligence, corruption, or incapacity . . . and when Thomas Jefferson failed in his policy disagreements and angry efforts to rid himself of Justice Salmon P. Chase.

U.S. history now provides us a line of clear precedent—particularly the first impeachment conviction, which centered on a judge incapable of intent ("insane" in the parlance of the day). A key portion of the Pickering impeachment articles provides a remarkably modern-sounding phrase: the judge was "guilty of other high misdemeanors . . . degrading to the honor and dignity of the United States."[325] The case established that no intent need be proved to convict; the criteria is harm and potential harm under "high Crimes and Misdemeanors."

THE MOST IMPORTANT LESSON: PARTICIPATE IN OUR DEMOCRACY. VOTE.

With love for my country and great hopes for the generations to come, the most important lesson this work reinforced is that a citizen's vote in congressional races is a most important vote. The U.S. citizen's vote every two years for our congressional House members (two-year terms) and senators (six-year terms, with approximately one-third up for reelection every two years) will put into office the front-line decision makers: Representatives who hold the power to investigate and decide whether to impeach and senators who will decide whether to acquit or convict and then, if convicted, whether to bar a convicted officer from again holding office.

What should citizens do? Register to vote. Vote. Tell your friends to vote, and tell your Congressperson how you feel. Learn the law of impeachment.

NOTES

1. In Britain, impeachment—now considered obsolete, per the House of Commons—was a means by which Parliament could prosecute and try individuals, normally holders of public office, for high treason or other crimes and misdemeanors. The first recorded impeachment in Parliament was in 1376 and the last in 1806. Impeachment in Britain has been replaced now with "other forms of accountability" as modern Britain understands that "the rules underpinning [British impeachment] have not been adapted to modern standards of democracy or procedural fairness." Caird, Jack Simpson, "Impeachment," Briefing Paper Number CBP7612, House of Commons Library (June 6, 2016), 3.

2. Governor Edmund Randolph, part of the Virginia delegation to the Constitutional Convention, who favored impeachment, warned that without impeachment: "Should no regular punishment be provided, it will be irregularly inflicted by tumults and insurrection." Doyle, Charles. "Impeachment Grounds: A Collection of Selected Materials" (Congressional Research Service, October 29, 1998), 9.

3. Alexander Hamilton in the Federalist papers No. 65 (1787) famously wrote that impeachment was designed as a "national inquest into the conduct of public men," and the subjects would be "those offenses which proceed from the misconduct of public men, or in other words, from the abuse or violation of some public trust. They are of a nature which may with peculiar propriety be "denominated POLITICAL, as they relate chiefly to injuries done immediately to the society itself" (emphasis in original). Hamilton, Alexander, James Madison, and John Jay. *The Federalist Papers* (Dover Thrift Edition.,Mineola, NY: Dover Publications), 2014, 318-19.

4. U.S. Congress Impeachment Inquiry Staff, Comm. on the Judiciary of the U.S. House of Representatives, 93rd Cong, Second Session, "Constitutional Grounds for Presidential Impeachment," 1974.

5. In U.S. impeachment practice, treachery and treasonous activity is pled as "other high Crimes and Misdemeanors" or generically as an "Impeachable Offense" rather than the harder-to-prove Constitutional "Treason." See, for example, the Humphreys case herein.

6. See the first impeachment conviction in U.S. history in Chapter 3 of this book: that of Judge Pickering, whose "insanity" was his uncontested defense. By 1803, when the House authorized impeachment, no one contested that he was incapable of forming the legal intent to commit his wrongdoings.

7. The impeachment conviction of the absent Judge Humphreys, who left his federal bench to wage war against the United States, was not pled as treason; the conviction required no proof of the elements of treason or intent to do wrong; the judge's motives were not even raised at trial, according to author William Lawrence. See Lawrence, William. "The Law of Impeachment," *American Law Register* 6 (1867): 679–80.

8. See generally the U.S. House of Representatives, Impeachment Inquiry Staff, Committee on the Judiciary of the U.S. House of Representatives, Constitutional Grounds for Presidential Impeachment staff report (hereafter cited as 1974 staff report) and its historical summary (26–7) showing that the emphasis has been on the significant effects of the conduct, emphasizing presidential impeachment, where "the crucial factor is not the intrinsic quality of behavior but the significance of its effect upon our constitutional system or the functioning of our government."

9. Common articles of U.S. impeachment allege the officer has violated his duties or oath or seriously undermined public confidence in his ability to perform his official functions. 1974 staff report, 21, with the emphasis on the significant effects of the conduct: undermining the integrity of office, disregard of constitutional duties and oath of office, arrogation of power, abuse of the governmental process, adverse impact on the system of government. 1974 staff report, 26.

10. 1974 staff report, 12–13, n. 56–77 and cases cited therein.

11. Black, Charles, *Impeachment: A Handbook* (New Haven and London, Yale University Press, 1974), 49–52. Professor Black conceded that some framers knew "a general way" of English usage of impeachment and that they borrowed the term "high Crimes and Misdemeanors," but did not concede any specialized knowledge: ". . . it is hard for me to think that many of them, or that many of the people at the state ratifying conventions, or many members of the late 18th-century American public" had specialized knowledge of the phrase "high Crimes and Misdemeanors." Black stated that English law, practice, and history, beginning in 1386 with the use of "high

Crimes and Misdemeanors," provided no guidance beyond the meaning of the phrase as "including serious misconduct in office," whether criminal or not. "Beyond that," he wrote, "I have to confess that I can read no clear message." With all due respect to Professor Black, the framers' words and explanations, in debate, in their published writings, in the state ratifying conventions as they taught the delegates what they knew, in their speeches in Congress, and in their lectures as law professors demonstrated their legal training in England and America, an appreciation for history, and their highly specialized knowledge and direction in debates and in such works as the Federalist papers on how their adaptation of the English law of "high Crimes and Misdemeanors" should be interpreted.

12. Berger, Raoul. *Impeachment: The Constitutional Problems* (Cambridge, Mass.: Harvard University Press, 1973), 30, n. 107, citing Quincy's Mass. Reports 1761–1772, Appendix IV, 581, 583–84.

13. The colonists' libraries contained British law books. Thomas Jefferson "combed debates in Parliament and the [English] State Trials" in his research of English law and practice, including impeachment law, for his famous "Manual of Parliamentary Practice" used for American proceedings. Of the fifty-five members of the federal Convention, nine had studied law in England. Berger, 87, n. 87, paragraphs 3 and 4.

14. Brown, H. Lowell, *High Crimes and Misdemeanors in Presidential Impeachment* (New York: Palgrave Macmillan, 2010), 25–26.

15. Doyle, *Impeachment Grounds*, 5.

16. Ibid., citing 2 *Wooddeson's Lectures* (1792 ed.), Lecture 40, pp. 596–597, 601, provides more information on Wooddeson's lectures and excerpts from the constitutional and ratifying conventions and the First Congress, well gathered and annotated by the fine researchers of the Congressional Research Service. See for example, Doyle, *Impeachment Grounds*, 5 et seq.; the House of Representatives inquiry into the impeachment of President Nixon produced their well-respected, sixty-page document summarizing the history and status of constitutional grounds for impeachment (1974 staff report).

17. Ibid., 5, citing 2 *Wooddeson's Lectures*, Lecture 40 (1792 ed.), 596 97, 601.

18. Although English kings and queens were determined to promote the idea that monarchs held a God given right to rule, Parliament—especially the House of Commons—used impeachment to challenge misconduct of the king's ministers and favorites and the idea of the king's absolute supremacy. See Berger, ch. 1, 30–33.

19. The English power to impeach, even if a king dissolved Parliament or pardoned the wrongdoer, promoted a political goal of denying the claim of absolute power of the king. Berger, p. 51.

20. King Charles I pronounced his absolute power to Parliament in

1626: "Parliaments are altogether in my power for the calling, sitting and dissolution. Therefore as I find the fruits of them to be good or evil, they are to continue or not to be." Berger, p. 31, citing Christopher Hill, *The Century of Revolution 1603–1714* (New York: Routledge, 1961), 73; and Peter Zagorin, *The Court and the Country*. (London: Atheneum, 1969), 87.

21. Perfidy: Act of violating faith, or one's vow or promise, or a trust; faithlessness; treachery. Madison also used the word *peculate*: to steal or misappropriate moneys, especially public moneys. *Webster's New Collegiate Dictionary*.

22. "Mr. Madison—thought it indispensable that some provision should be made for defending the Community agst the incapacity, negligence or perfidy of the chief Magistrate. The limitation of the period of his service, was not a sufficient security. He might lose his capacity after his appointment. He might pervert his administration into a scheme of peculation or oppression. He might betray his trust to foreign powers . . . In the case of the Executive Magistracy which was to be administered by a single man, loss of capacity or corruption was more within the compass of probable events, and either of them might be fatal to the Republic." Doyle, *Impeachment Grounds*, 8, citing James Madison, *Notes of Debates in the Federal Convention of 1787* (New York: Norton, 1987), 332–33.

23. The Declaration of Independence summarized the "History of the present King of Great-Britain" acting with the object of "an absolute Tyranny over these States." The Declaration made clear that the kings' governors, judges, and "swarms of Officers" in America did not answer to the colonists or their efforts to legislate. The colonist's complaints against the king included:

- Refusing "to Assent to Laws, the most wholesome and necessary for the public Good."
- Forbidding "his Governors to pass Laws of immediate and pressing Importance, unless suspended in their Operation till his Assent should be obtained; and when so suspended, he has utterly neglected to attend to them."
- Refusing "to pass other Laws for the Accommodation of large Districts of People, unless those People would relinquish the Right of Representation in the Legislature, a Right inestimable to them, and formidable to Tyrants only."
- Dissolving "Representative Houses repeatedly, for opposing with manly Firmness his Invasions on the Rights of the People."
- Obstructing "the Administration of Justice by refusing his Assent to Laws for establishing Judiciary Powers."

- Making "the Military independent of and superior to the Civil Power."
- Making "Judges dependent on his Will alone, for the Tenure of their Offices, and the Amount and Payment of their Salaries."
- Erecting a "Multitude of new Offices and sent hither Swarms of Officers to harass our People and eat out their Substance."
- Cutting off U.S. "Trade with all Parts of the World."
- Allowing others to make laws of "pretended Legislation" and "suspending" the colonial "Legislatures" that should be writing the laws.

Declaration of Independence, 1776. See also Berger, 5.

24. Berger, 5, "Governor and Judges had been saddled on the Colonists by the King or his minions."

25. Ibid., 4–5.

26. Ibid., 4, n. 25, 26, and accompanying text; Ibid., 99, n. 216.

27. Gouverneur Morris contributed multiple ideas to the U.S. Constitutional Convention, which he attended as a delegate from Pennsylvania. Morris had helped promote the Revolution's cause in New York, helped write New York's first constitution and, although called away from the U.S. Constitutional Convention, was asked to perform much of the polishing work in stylistic rewriting of the Constitution. He is credited with the wording of the Preamble of the Constitution. Whitney, David C, *Founders of Freedom in America; Lives of the Men Who Signed the Constitution* (Chicago: J. G. Ferguson, 1965), 158, 161–62.

We the People of the United States, in Order to form a more perfect Union, establish Justice, insure domestic Tranquility, provide for the common defence, promote the general Welfare, and secure the Blessings of Liberty to ourselves and our Posterity, do ordain and establish this Constitution for the United States of America.

U.S. Constitution. Preamble.

28. Doyle, *Impeachment Grounds*, 9.

29. The Secret Treaty of Dover (1670) was a deal separate from a formal treaty made by King Charles II of England with King Louis XIV of France. Charles II of England was to receive money and troop support, if necessary, for his use when he declared himself a Roman Catholic (which didn't happen), with further moneys for joining in war against the Dutch. Charles II agreed that England would support Louis XIV of France in any claims Louis might have to Spanish succession. "Treaty of Dover England-France 1670." Accessed April 12, 2017: https://www.britannica.com/event/Treaty-

of-Dover. The promise, by a king of England to convert to what was "regarded by most English people for a hundred years as the bitterest enemy of their own church" was extraordinary. Hutton, R. *The Making of the Secret Treaty of Dover, 1668–1670* (Cambridge: Cambridge University Press), 1986. Abstract accessed May 14, 2017: http://www.jstor.org/stable/2639064.

The reference by Morris to the Secret Treaty is found at Doyle, *Impeachment Grounds*, 9, citing II Farrand 64–9 (Madison). Farrand's three-volume *The Records of the Federal Convention of 1787* was published in New Haven by Yale University Press in 1966 per H. Lowell Brown, 225; *The Records* are a chronologically arranged collection of notes of the various delegates (primarily Madison), per Doyle, *Impeachment Grounds*, 7, n. 6.

Despite Morris's wit giving him a tendency to shoot from the hip, President Washington appointed Morris his Minister to France. Morris witnessed the great tumults of the French Revolution. He unsuccessfully attempted to obtain the release of Washington's dear friend the Marquis de Lafayette. New York governor DeWitt Clinton eulogized his friend Morris in 1816: "[h]e united wit, logic, pathos and intelligence." Whitney, David C., *Founders of Freedom . . . Constitution*, 162–63.

30. See generally Berger, ch. 1, "The Parliamentary Power to Declare Retrospective Treasons," 8–17 regarding the salvo, and 7–52 explaining English history and use of treason law, and for examples of the fluid concept of treason, 33–34. Berger explains in detail the famous impeachment of the Earl of Stratford, carrying diverse treason theories, "a great watershed in English constitutional history of which the Founders were aware." Ibid., 30, n. 7.

31. English impeachment carried criminal penalties, including death. Treason under English impeachment was a fluid concept, and Parliament could declare a treason retroactively. Berger, 8–13; see Doyle, *Impeachment Grounds*, 2–4, citing Blackstone, *Commentaries on the Laws of England*, 126–28 (1769). Commoners, too, could be impeached before the lords, but only for "high misdemeanors," not for capital offenses (punishable by death). Doyle, *Impeachment Grounds*, 4.

32. The Founding Fathers, familiar with impeachment in their state constitutions, understood American impeachment as "a bridle in the hands of the legislative body upon the executive servants of the government." Federalist 65, 320.

33. Berger, 5.

34. Under the U.S. Constitution, the Americans explicitly barred any federal or state *ex post facto* law (U.S. Const. Art. I, Sec. 9, Clause 3; Art. I, Sec. 10, Clause 1) and prohibited Bills of Attainder (an act declaring a

group of people guilty, and then proceeding to punish them) in Art.
I, Sec. 9. The United States grants no noble titles without Congress
agreeing, and the president may not take any present, emolument,
office, or title from any king, prince, or foreign state (U.S. Const. Art.
I, Sec. 9, Clause 8); the president cannot receive any emolument from
the states (Art. II, Sec. 1, Clause 7). A presidential veto checks the legislative power of Congress, but Congress may override the veto (U.S.
Const. Art. I, Sec. 7, Clause 2). A president may not pardon in cases of
impeachment. U.S. Const. Art. II, Sec. 2, Clause 1, allows presidential
pardons "except in Cases of Impeachment."

35. See Berger, 8. British treason law included the terms "levying war
against . . ., or adhering to his enemies."

36. U.S. Const. Art. III, Sec. 3, Clause 1.

37. The president, according to the earlier draft language: "shall be
removed from office on impeachment by the House of Representatives, and conviction by the Senate, for Treason, or bribery." Doyle,
Impeachment Grounds, 10. The clause would represent a change
from British law in several ways. In the proposed U.S. impeachment clause at issue in Philadelphia at the Constitutional Convention, impeachment was no longer applicable to everyone, as it was
in Britain; U.S. impeachment applied only to public officers. The
Americans had eliminated the criminality element, and eliminated
the application to anyone other than "officers of the U.S.," in addition to eliminating the clause (known as "the salvo") that allowed
the determination of English treason to be made after the fact.
See Berger, 16–20. "The Framers were highly conscious they were
writing a document for posterity." Berger, 123, n. 8.

38. Brown, H. Lowell, 5, text and accompanying notes 21, 22, and 23,
citing James Madison, *Notes of Debates in the Federal Convention of
1787* (New York: Norton, 1987).

39. The Hastings trial, in progress during the Constitutional Convention, included "high Crimes and Misdemeanors," gross maladministration, corruption in office, and "cruelty towards the people of
India." 1974 staff report, 7.

40. 1974 staff report, 7. The famous, short impeachment debate resulting in the choice of the Impeachment Clause language, allows us
to eavesdrop on legendary Founding Fathers Mason, Madison, and
Morris talking about the "avidly" followed British impeachment trial
of Governor-General Warren Hastings, as the Constitutional Convention attendees worked in Philadelphia. As the U.S. Senate website
explains: "Even as the Constitution's framers toiled in Philadelphia
in 1787, the impeachment trial of British official Warren Hastings
was in progress in London and avidly followed in America. Hastings,

who was eventually acquitted, was charged with oppression, bribery, and fraud as colonial administrator and first governor-general in India." U.S. Senate website, "Impeachment." Accessed March 9, 2017: https://www.senate.gov/artandhistory/history/common/briefing/Senate_Impeachment_Role.htm.

41. The famous debate excerpt reads as follows: "'The clause referring to the Senate, the trial of impeachments agst. The President, for Treason & bribery, was taken up.

"'Col. Mason. Why is the provision restrained to Treason & bribery only? Treason as defined in the Constitution will not reach many great and dangerous offences. Hastings is not guilty of Treason. Attempts to subvert the Constitution may not be Treason as above defined—As bills of attainder which have saved the British Constitution are forbidden, it is the more necessary to extend: the power of impeachments.' He moved to add after 'bribery' or 'maladministration.' Mr. Gerry seconded him—

"'Mr Madison So vague a term will be equivalent to a tenure during pleasure of the Senate.

"'Mr Govr Morris, it will not be put in force & can do no harm— An election of every four years will prevent maladministration.

"'Col. Mason withdrew 'maladministration' & substitutes 'other high crimes & misdemeanors'<agst. the State'>

"'On the question thus altered [the Convention agreed].

"'In the amendment of Col. Mason just agreed to, the word 'State' after the words [']misdemeanors against' was struck out, and the words 'United States' inserted, <unanimously> in order to remove ambiguity—

"'On the question to agree to clause as amended, [the Convention agreed]

"'On motion 'The vice-President and other Civil officers and the U.S. shall be removed from office on impeachment and conviction as aforesaid' was added to the clause on the subject of impeachments.

"'A Committee was then appointed by Ballot to revise the stile of and arrange the articles which had been agreed to by the House." Doyle, *Impeachment Grounds*, 10–11, n. 7–9; See also Black, 28; Simpson, 18; Berger, 163, n. 183. For a discussion and acceptance of the Committee of Style's faithful work, capturing the intent of the framers and the vote to approve, see *Nixon v. United States*, 506 U.S. 224, 231 (1993).

42. Mason didn't sign the Constitution, siding with the anti-Federalists and seeking more concessions for the Southern states. Mason was insulted—as was Patrick Henry—by Federalists referring to their

absence from active military service in the War of Independence. Alden, John, *George Washington: A Biography* (New York and Avenel: Wings Books, 1984), 227. See also Alden, 106 (preparation of militia with George Washington) and 232–33 (detailing the contest over the Constitution marked by strong language, minor mob action, and rancor left over from the struggle for ratification).

43. Morison, Samuel Eliot, *The Oxford History of the American People* (New York: Oxford University Press, 1965), 271; Ellis, Joseph, *His Excellency: George Washington* (New York: Alfred A. Knopf, 2004), 62–63.

44. On Mason and his role in the Virginia constitution, see Brown, 12; Morison, 221.

45. Morison, 221, 272.

46. Whitney, *Founders of Freedom . . . Constitution*, 236.

47. 1974 staff report, 16, and 9, and accompanying n. 31. The staff noted that " . . . the impeachability of the President was considered to be an important element of his responsibility."

48. Whitney, *Founders of Freedom . . . Constitution*, 231–35.

49. James Wilson vigorously debated against a system involving a three-man executive proposal, in favor of his single-executive proposal. History can credit Wilson's forceful debating with the 7–3 vote favoring one chief executive. Whitney, *Founders of Freedom . . . Constitution*, 232. It was Wilson, too, who argued strongly, persuasively, and effectively against use of "wealth" for criteria in reapportionment for the House of Representatives. Whitney, *Founders of Freedom . . . Constitution*, 235–236.

50. Hamilton wrote that the model for the American impeachment process—trying public men for the "abuse or violation of some public trust"—was "borrowed[.] . . . In Great Britain it is the province of the House of Commons to prefer the impeachment and of the House of Lords to decide upon it." Federalist 65, pars. 2, 5.

51. Chernow, Ronald, *Washington: A Life* (New York: Penguin, 2010), 204, 291–292, 442, 598.

52. Hamilton accomplished much in a life cut short by his political criticism of Aaron Burr, leading to a quarrel and Hamilton's death following his fatal injury in a duel with Burr. George Washington wrote of Hamilton: "That he is ambitious I shall readily grant, but it is of that laudable kind which prompts a man to excel in whatever he takes in hand. He is enterprising, quick in his perception, and his judgment is intuitively great . . ." Whitney, *Founders of Freedom . . . Constitution*, 105–09.

53. Hamilton et al., *The Federalist Papers*, Federalist 65. Hamilton, a self-made man who borrowed money to come to America to attend college, spoke eloquently defending the patriots dumping tea

in Boston Harbor, published well-respected pamphlets, and volunteered for the War of Independence.

Hamilton literally had George Washington's back; a captain of artillery, "[h]is company fought in the rear guard in the retreat of the Continental Army from Long Island. Whitney, *Founders of Freedom . . . Constitution*, 107. He saw action in battle at White Plains, Trenton, and Princeton, and later, at Yorktown, after service as aide-de-camp to General Washington. Ibid., 105–107. Hamilton, Washington's "most gifted scribe," had impressed his general with his artillery work at White Plains and the Raritan River. Chernow, 292–293. Washington greatly valued Hamilton's judgment. Whitney, *Founders of Freedom . . . Constitution*, 105–09.

54. Federalist 65, pars. 5–8. Hamilton discussed judicial power of the Senate, explaining the rationale of having the Senate "dignified" and "independent," impartial and confident in its own situation (par. 6) to try the impeachment case, citing in paragraph five the English model, and the fact that several State constitutions follow the example, regarding "the practice of impeachment as a bridle in the hands of the legislative body upon the executive servants of the government." Federalist No. 65, par. 5.

In pars. 8 and 9, Hamilton addresses the reasoning for not utilizing the Supreme Court, or some other entity for the trial, while still obtaining the benefits of union with the Supreme Court by using its chief justice to preside over the court of impeachment. Hamilton continues to address the objections to use of the Senate in Federalist 66, defending the use of a legislative body for a judicial function, dividing the right of accusing to the House and the right of judging to the Senate in Federalist 66, par. 2.

Here Hamilton continues to acknowledge the objection that impeachment places much power in the Senate, but finds the objection too imprecise, and he continues his justifications for his confidence in the Senate, emphasizing the duration of their terms, and the balance of other powers into the House, for example, the exclusive origination of money bills and the sole power to institute impeachment. Federalist 66, pars. 4–7. He also acknowledges—and defends—the power and role of the Senate providing advice and consent "in the business of appointments." Federalist 66, pars. 8–9.

Of great interest is Hamilton's emphasis on the "security essentially intended by the Constitution against corruption and treachery in the formation of treaties," in paragraph 12 of Federalist 66. In Federalist 65, par. 7, he previously recognized the "awful discretion" lying with the Senate in impeachment, which forbids trusting impeachment power to a "small number of persons." In Federalist

66, in concluding par. 13, Hamilton reinforces the idea that the Senate should be allowed massive powers involving treaties as well as trying impeachment cases, as a collective body, to serve "the public good." Hamilton emphasizes a hope and trust that the Senate will do right in the treaty-making as well as impeachment arena:

"So far as might concern the misbehavior of the executive in perverting the instructions or contravening the views of the Senate, we need not be apprehensive of the want of disposition in that body to punish or abuse of their confidence or to vindicate their own authority. We may thus count upon their pride, if not upon their virtue."

Hamilton admits the system devised may not be perfect, but the lack of perfection would not justify rejection of the Constitution, embracing the idea of the institution of government:

"If mankind were to resolve to agree in no institution of government, until every part of it had been adjusted to the most exact standard of perfection, society would soon become a general scene of anarchy, and the world a desert."

Federalist 65, par. 10.

55. Doyle, *Impeachment Grounds*, 12. See also 1974 staff report, 15.

56. For historical dates and events see U.S. Congress, *Constitution with Index and Declaration of Independence*, 108th Cong., 1st sess, H. Doc. 108-96, 40. For Madison's intent that some level of maladministration serve as "other high Crimes and Misdemeanors" for impeachment, see Brown, 35–36.

57. Whitney, *Founders of Freedom . . . Constitution*, 141–142.

58. Brown, 35, citing Gates, Joseph ed. *The Debates and Proceedings in the Congress of the United States*, vol. 1 (Washington, DC: Gales and Seaton, 1834), 495–496.

59. "The danger, then, consists merely in this—the President can displace from office a man whose merits require that he should be continued in it. What will be the motives which the President can feel for such abuse of his power, and the restraints that operate to prevent it? In the first place, he will be impeachable by this house, before the Senate, for such an act of maladministration; for I contend that the wanton removal of a meritorious officer would subject him to impeachment and removal from his own high trust." Doyle, *Impeachment Grounds*, 12; see also 1974 staff report, 15.

60. Madison was supported in his congressional speech by another framer, Abraham Baldwin of Georgia:

Mr. Baldwin: If the President, "in a fit of passion" removed "all the good officers of government" and the Senate were unable to choose successors, the consequences would be

that the President "would be obligated to do the duties himself; or if he did not, we would impeach him, and turn him
out of office, as he had others."

1974 staff report, 15.

61. Whitney, *Founders of Freedom . . . Constitution*, 141.

62. Whitney, *Founders of Freedom . . . Constitution*, 146.

63. Bazan, *Impeachment: An Overview of Constitutional Provisions, Procedure and Practice*, Congressional Research Service, 2010, 9, n. 38–39.
The president can provide information to Congress, as did President Adams in the case of Senator Blount's treachery. President
Adams forwarded information and documents exposing Blount's
involvement in the plan to stir Native Americans into hostilities
with Spain, and other actions in violation of U.S. neutrality. Brown,
p. 37. President Thomas Jefferson provided to Congress the information on Judge John Pickering's misconduct, gathered by the
president's secretary of the treasury Albert Gallatan and U.S. Attorney Samuel Sherburne. Brown, 40. Outside groups or individuals also may supply information leading to impeachment activities.
In 1932, the House of Representatives learned of allegations against
federal judge Harold Louderback from a petition from the Bar
Association of San Francisco alleging the judge appointed friends
and allies to receivership positions. The petition led to hearings by
an investigative committee, which recommended impeachment
to the House Judiciary Committee, which instead recommended
only censure. The House of Representatives, however, voted to impeach. The Senate acquitted Judge Louderback.

64. *Nixon v. United States*, 506 U.S., 224, 228–38. Chief Justice Rehnquist
also noted the harms, including lack of finality, particularly if the
president were impeached, to months or years of chaos during judicial review or retrial, with a different Senate, and the great dif-
ficulty of fashioning judicial review of the Senate's impeachment
verdict. *Nixon v. United States*, 236.

65. *Nixon v. United States*, 224, 233 (1993).

66. *Nixon v. United States*, 224 (1993); Bazan, *Overview of Constitutional
Provisions*, 1–6, discusses in detail twenty-first-century impeachment processes under House and Senate rules in two twenty-
first-century impeachment proceedings. Rule XI of the "Rules of
Procedure and Practice in the Senate when Sitting on Impeachment
Trials" enables creation of a trial committee. In making determi-
nations in an impeachment trial, the Senate may rely on evidence
gathered by a Senate impeachment trial committee or gather further evidence. Bazan, *Overview of Constitutional Provisions*, 3–4.

67. Bazan, *Overview of Constitutional Provisions*, 10, n. 40.

68. Cole, Jared and Todd Garvey. *Impeachment: Grounds for Removal.* Congressional Research Service, 2015, i ("Summary"). See also Bazan, *Overview of Constitutional Provisions,* 20–21, providing examples and the possible significance of *United States v. Mouat,* 124 U.S. 303 (1888) stating that, absent appointment, federal judgeship, or service as head of department, an individual is not "strictly speaking" an officer of the United States in interacting with the Appointments Clause of the Constitution, Art. II, Sec. 2., Clause 2, buttressing the argument that, at least, impeachment covers officers appointed in accordance with the Appointments Clause. For a massive list of investigations, impeachment resolution, and inquiries involving judges or executive branch persons or officers that did not culminate in impeachment in the House. See Bazan, *Overview of Constitutional Provisions,* 18–20.

69. See impeachment cases in Chapter 2 herein of Judges Claiborne, W. Nixon, and Kent each criminally convicted, which conviction did not prevent impeachment and impeachment convictions (Claiborne and W. Nixon) or resignation (Kent), and impeachment of Judge Alcee Hastings, whose acquittal did not prevent impeachment and conviction.

70. Federalist 65, par. 8.

71. The 1974 staff report from the Watergate impeachment investigation is consistent with the intent of the Founding Fathers, as the report made clear:

> "It would be anomalous if the framers, having barred criminal sanctions from the impeachment remedy and limited it to removal and possible disqualification from office, intended to restrict the grounds to conduct that was criminal."

1974 staff report, 27.

72. Rehnquist, William H. *Grand Inquests: The Historic Impeachments of Samuel Chase and President Andrew Johnson.* New York: William Morrow, 1992, 274. U.S. Supreme Court Chief Justice Rehnquist, in praising the House Judiciary Committee, noted that "the preparation and spotlight of the Nixon Watergate Impeachment" produced "much reasoned discussion, both within and without the Committee, as to the nature of Impeachment. All members of the Judiciary Committee—even the ten Republicans who voted no on each proposed article— appear to have rejected the view that a constitutional 'high crime or misdemeanor' must be an indictable offense under the criminal law."

73. See Bazan, *Overview of Constitutional Provisions,* generally and 10, 22; see cases of Judges Pickering, W. Nixon, and Kent. Does Hamilton's word "after" Federalist 65, par. 8 mean that a president—or

any official—may be temporarily immune from prosecution? The answer is no as to judges, probably no as to anyone other than the president, and debated as to the president.

Scholars have long debated whether the president should be immune—while in office—from indictment and conviction, using a variety of arguments, including the "after" language of Alexander Hamilton in Federalist 65, par. 8 ("After having been sentenced . . ."). Compare Moss, Randolph. Assistant Attorney General, Office of Legal Counsel, "A Sitting President's Amenability to Indictment and Criminal Prosecution." Oct. 16, 2000. Moss; Freedman, Eric M. "On Protecting Accountability." 27 *Hofstra Law Review*: Iss. 4, 1999.

Moss, in a Department of Justice memorandum in 2000 reaffirming a 1973 memorandum argues that the president should not be tied up with the criminal process. Freedman argues that, if "Law is King" (and not, as in ancient Britain, king is law), then a sitting president should be treated as any other person. He notes that Vice President Aaron Burr was indicted in office for the murder of Alexander Hamilton, with Founding Fathers still alive and not objecting. Yet Freedman concedes that the Founding Fathers were clearly divided on the issue at the time of the Constitutional and state ratifying conventions with no clear Constitutional-era original intent; the issue was discussed and argued, put off, and never resolved.

Clearly, sitting judges have been indicted and convicted, remaining in office, then impeached and convicted under the Impeachment Clause. Some claimed immunity. Freedman details the judges' claims rejected on appeal, with the Supreme Court declining to revisit/hear the appeal.

Moss argues that the presidency is different from any other office. The Clinton impeachment activity and actions by the House managers, citing judicial impeachment cases as clear, usable precedent, confirmed that there is one constitutional standard for judges and a president, not two, for impeachment: "high Crimes and Misdemeanors," as this *Citizen's Guide* explains.

Nonetheless, the question remains open as to whether the president is so important as to be treated differently than every other sitting officer of the United States. Indeed, in the Clinton impeachment, the prosecution argued that the president's massive duties and powers (e.g., as head of the Department of Justice and thereby law enforcement) increased his responsibility for impeachable acts, such as lying and undermining faith in the administration of justice.

74. In the impeachment of Samuel Kent, the House members took pains

to note that, while this case certainly involved criminal conduct, impeachment did not require a crime. The House Resolution H. Rep. 111-159, sess. of 2001, pertaining to Judge Kent contained "A Brief Discussion of Impeachment," specifically citing the House Report accompanying the Resolutions to Impeach Judges Nixon and Hasting concerning the meaning of "high Crimes and Misdemeanors," noting that impeachment is "non criminal" and serves "simply to remove the offender from office" and that impeachment is "the ultimate means of preserving our constitutional form of government from the depredations of those who abuse or violate the public trust."

H.R. 520, 111th Cong., citing H. Rep. 101-36 (1989), Impeachment of Walter L. Nixon, Jr., Report of the Committee on the Judiciary to Accompany H.R. Res. 87, 101st Cong., 5; and H. Rep. 100-810 (1988), Impeachment of Alcee L. Hastings, Report of the Committee on the Judiciary to accompany H.R. Res. 499, 100th Cong., 6. The "Brief Discussion of Impeachment" then concluded by reemphasizing, recognizing the criminal nature of Judge Kent's misconduct, that: ". . . the principles that underpin the propriety of impeachment do not require the conduct of issue be criminal in nature, or that there have been a criminal prosecution." Ibid.

75. Report Accompanying H.R. 520, 111th Cong., citing H. Rep. 101-36 (1989), Impeachment of Walter L. Nixon, Jr., Report of the Committee on the Judiciary to Accompany H.R. Res. 87, 101st Cong., 5; and H. Rep. 100-810 (1988), Impeachment of Alcee L. Hastings, Report of the Committee on the Judiciary to accompany H.R. Res. 499, 100th Cong., 6. Sections 2.1 and 2.2 provide more background and proof on this issue. See also H. Rep. 111–159, sess. of 2009, Impeachment of Judge Samuel B. Kent.

76. Report Accompanying H.R. Res. 520, 111th Cong., citing H. Rep. 101-36 (1989), Impeachment of Walter L. Nixon, Jr., Report of the Committee on the Judiciary to Accompany H.R. Res. 87, 101st Cong., 5; and H. Rep. 100-810 (1988), Impeachment of Alcee L. Hastings, Report of the Committee on the Judiciary to accompany H.R. Res. 499, 100th Cong., 6. See also H. Rep. 111–59, sess. of 2009, Impeachment of Judge Samuel B. Kent.

77. "No Title of Nobility shall be granted by the United States: And no Person holding any Office of Profit or Trust under them, shall, without the Consent of the Congress, accept of any present, Emolument, Office or Title, of any kind whatever, from any King, Prince, or foreign State." U.S. Const. Art. I, Sec. 9, Clause 8. The Constitution prohibits any state from granting "any Title or Nobility" in Article I, Section 10.

78. "The President shall, at stated Times, receive for his Services, a Com-

pensation, which shall neither be increased nor diminished during the Period for which he shall have been elected, and he shall not receive within that Period any other Emolument from the United States, or any of them." U.S. Const. Art. II, Sec. 1, Clause 7.

79. Federalist 65.

80. 1974 staff report, 27.

81. Doyle, *Impeachment Grounds*, 5, citing 2 *Wooddeson's Lectures*, Lecture 40, 596–97, 601 (1792 ed.). The Founding Fathers kept that goal—preventing injury to the commonwealth—but improved and modernized the ancient impeachment system to permit peaceful removal—without criminal punishment—of their president, maintaining the integrity of our government. The Americans gave the people the rights denied to English people of the eighteenth century, who had no power to impeach and remove their king; he wielded absolute power.

82. See Doyle, *Impeachment Grounds*, 8, reproducing discussions of impeachment at the Constitutional Convention.

83. See Doyle, *Impeachment Grounds*, 8–9, reproducing discussions of impeachment at the Constitutional Convention.

84. Cole and Garvey: https://fas.org/sgp/crs/misc/R44260.pdf, 9, citing Brown, W., *House Practice: A Guide to the Rules, Precedents, and Procedures of the House*, ch. 27, sec. 4 (2011). Committee on the Judiciary, 93d Cong., *Impeachment—Selected Material* 692 (comm. print 1973), 666; Brown, W., *House Practice: A Guide to the Rules, Precedents, and Procedures of the House*, ch. 27 §1 (2011); *Impeachment of William Jefferson Clinton*, H. Rep. 105-830 at 110–18 (1998). Committee on the Judiciary, *Constitutional Grounds for Presidential Impeachment*, Report of the Staff of the Impeachment Inquiry, U.S. House of Representatives, 105th Cong. 2d sess. (1998); Brown, 104.

85. U.S. Const. Art. III, Sec. 1.

86. "The judicial Power of the United States, shall be vested in one supreme Court, and in such inferior Courts as the Congress may from time to time ordain and establish. The Judges, both of the supreme and inferior Courts, shall hold their Offices during good Behaviour, and shall, at stated Times, receive for their Services, a Compensation, which shall not be diminished during their Continuance in Office." U.S. Const. Art. III, Sec. 1.

87. The clear law is that U.S. constitutional impeachment is governed by the Impeachment Clause. The phrase "good behavior" is viewed as a designation of judicial tenure with one standard for both judges and executive branch officers. "[A] 1973 discussion of impeachment grounds released by the House Judiciary Committee reviewed the history of the phrase and concluded that the 'Consti-

tutional Convention . . . quite clearly rejected' a 'dual standard' for judges and civil officers." Cole and Garvey, 9–10, n. 74; see also Cole and Garvey, 9, citing Brown, W., *House Practice: A Guide to the Rules, Precedents, and Procedures of the House*, ch. 27, sec. 4 (2011). Committee on the Judiciary, 93d Cong., *Impeachment—Selected Material* 692 (comm. print 1973), p. 666; Brown, W., *House Practice: A Guide to the Rules, Precedents, and Procedures of the House*, ch. 27 §1 (2011); *Impeachment of William Jefferson Clinton*, H. Rep. 105-830 at 110–18 (1998). Committee on the Judiciary, *Constitutional Grounds for Presidential Impeachment*, Report of the Staff of the Impeachment Inquiry, U.S. House of Representatives, 105th Cong. 2d sess. (1998); Brown, 104.

88. Cole and Garvey, 9–10, citing Committee on the Judiciary, 93d Cong., *Impeachment—Selected Material* 692 (comm. print 1973), 666; Brown, W., *House Practice: A Guide to the Rules, Precedents, and Procedures of the House* ch. 27 §1 (2011); *Impeachment of William Jefferson Clinton*, H. Rep. 105-830, at 110–18 (1998).

89. Brown, 104; see Committee on the Judiciary, *Constitutional Grounds for Presidential Impeachment*, Report of the Staff of the Impeachment Inquiry, U.S. House of Representatives, 105th Cong. 2d sess. (1998).

90. Fernandez, Justin. *High Crimes and Misdemeanors: The Impeachment Process*. Philadelphia: Chelsea House Publishers, 2001, 96. While it is "devastating" for the judiciary when judges are perceived as dishonest, the report argued, perjury by the president was "just as devastating to our system of government." Cole and Garvey, 9–10, citing H. Rep. 105-830, at 113 (1998).

91. 1974 staff report, 27.

92. Bazan, *Overview of Constitutional Provisions*, 24, citing H. Rep. 101-36, at 5 (1989), also quoted in H. Rep. 111-159, at 5 (2009).

93. 1974 staff report, 21.

94. U.S. Const. Art. II, Sec. 1, Clause 8 (Oath); Art. II, Sec. 3 ("Take Care" clause).

95. A presidential veto checks the legislative power of Congress, but Congress may override the veto. U.S. Const. Art. I, Sec. 7, Clause 2.

96. Pardon power is broad, and the only limits mentioned in the Constitution are: pardons are limited to offenses against the United States—that is, not state or civil cases—and "they cannot affect an impeachment process." Pardons have great use: Founding Father James Wilson stated, "pardon before conviction might be necessary in order to obtain the testimony of accomplices." Pfiffner, James. "The President's Broad Power to Pardon and Commute." The Heritage Foundation, July 7, 2007, 2–5; *Schick v. Reed* 419 U.S. 256 (1974) (affirming power of President Eisenhower's addition of "no parole" in a commutation of a death sentence to life sentence, at hard labor,

dishonorable discharge and forfeiture of pay, on condition of no parole; the Court makes clear the Founding Fathers' knowledge of English law: "familiarity with the English law and practice," and stating ". . . the conclusion is inescapable that the pardoning power was intended to commute sentences on conditions which do not, in themselves, offend the Constitution, but which are not specifically provided for by statute.") *Schick v. Reed* 419 U.S., 263–64.

97. 1974 staff report, 13–14.

98. Regarding "substantiality," see 1974 staff report generally, and 21, 26. Regarding pardons: Several authors have given examples of single acts warranting impeachment, particularly abuse of pardons. For example, since the Constitution Art. II, Sec. 2, Clause 1, allows presidential pardons "except in Cases of Impeachment," an unconstitutional pardoning has been described as impeachable, as have wanton acts of guaranteeing pardons in advance under unjustified circumstances. One extreme hypothetical referenced an offensive, hypothetical policy for pardons promised in advance for any federal agents or police killing anyone in the District of Columbia in the line of duty, however unnecessary the killing. Black, 34.

99. See Pfiffner, 2; 1974 staff report, 21, 26.

100. Doyle, *Impeachment Grounds*, 5 cites Blackstone on bribery: Bribery is the next species of offense against public justice; it is when a judge, or other person concerned in the administration of justice, takes any undue reward to influence his behavior and his office. For bribery by statute see for example, 18 USC Sec. 201 "Bribery of Public Officials and Witnesses," U.S. Department of Justice, Office of the United States Attorneys, U.S. Attorneys Manual [USAM], Sec. 2041: https://www.justice.gov/usam.

Treason under the U.S. Constitution is very narrowly defined. "Treason against the United States, shall consist only in levying War against them, or in adhering to their enemies, giving them Aid and Comfort." The Constitution provides rules providing that: "No person shall be convicted of Treason unless on the Testimony of two Witnesses to the same overt Act, or on Confession in open Court." U.S. Const. Art. III, Sec. 3, Clause 1.

101. See cases of Judges Humphreys and English, and secretary of war Belknap.

102. See cases of Presidents Johnson, Nixon, and Clinton; and Judges Johnson, Pickering, and Blount.

103. 1974 staff report, 18–21, 26.

104. Acting to "defeat the claims of the United States . . .": Pickering, per Impeachment Art. I, acted "contrary to his trust and duty as judge of the said district court." Simpson, Appendix at 193. Art. II

complained of Judge Pickering's refusal to hear the testimony of the U.S. Attorney's witnesses, ready to prove the forfeiture right of the United States to the vessel, as the Judge acted "with the intent to defeat the just claims of the United States," ordering the vessel restored to Eliphat Ladd, "contrary to his [Pickering's] trust and duty."

105. George Mason and James Madison in the Virginia Ratifying Convention, cited in 1974 staff report, 13, including Mason's comment: The president might use his pardoning power to "pardon crimes which were advised against himself" or before indictment or conviction "to stop inquiry and prevent detection."

Madison: "[I]f the President be connected, in any suspicious manner, with any person, and there be grounds to believe he will shelter him, the House of Representatives can impeach him; they can remove him if found guilty."

106. The Clinton Impeachment Articles (in paragraphs three of each of the two Articles) specifically asserted he had undermined integrity of the office, "brought disrepute on the Presidency, has betrayed his trust as President and has acted in a manner subversive of the rule of law and justice, to the manifest injury of the people of the United States." Brown, 157-159. The Nixon proposed Impeachment Articles 1 and 2, each concluded: "In all of this, Richard M. Nixon has acted in a manner contrary to his trust as President and subversive of constitutional government, to the great prejudice of the cause of justice and to the manifest injury of the United States." *Impeachment Articles*, Brown, 153–54. Nixon Proposed Article 3 (regarding refusal to produce subpoenaed items) stated "In all of this Richard Nixon has acted in a manner contrary to his trust as President and subversive of constitutional government . . ." Brown, 156.

107. James Madison in debate on need for Impeachment Clause: "[The president] might betray his trust to foreign powers." To Madison, loss of capacity or corruption "might be fatal to the republic." Brown, 5–6, quoting James Madison, *Notes of Debates in the Federal Convention of 1787* (New York: Norton), 1987, 332–33.

Gouverneur Morris at Constitutional Convention: "Mr.Govr. Morris's opinion had been changed by the arguments used in the discussion. He was now sensible of the necessity of impeachments, if the Executive was to continue for any time in office. Our Executive was not like a Magistrate having a life interest, much less like one having an hereditary interest in his office. He may be bribed by a greater interest to betray his trust; and no *one would say that we ought to expose ourselves to the danger of seeing the first Magistrate in foreign pay without being able to guard agst it by displacing him.*" Doyle, *Impeachment Grounds*, 9 (emphasis added).

From Wooddeson, English impeachment law on examples of
impeachable abuses, including trust betrayal: "Such kind of mis-
deeds however as peculiarly injure the commonwealth by the
abuse of high offices of trust, are the most proper and have been
the most usual grounds for this kind of prosecution. Thus, if a lord
chancellor be guilty of bribery, or of acting grossly contrary to the
duty of his office, if the judges mislead their sovereign by unconstitutional opinions, if any other magistrate attempt to subvert the
fundamental laws, or introduce arbitrary power, these have been
deemed cases adapted to parliamentary inquiry and decision. So
where a lord chancellor has been thought to have put the seal to an
ignominious treaty, a lord admiral to neglect the safeguard of the
sea, an ambassador *to betray his trust*, a privy counselor to propound
or support pernicious and dishonorable measures, or a confidential advisor of his sovereign to obtain exorbitant grants or incompatible employments, these imputations have properly occasioned
impeachments; because it is apparent how little the ordinary tribunals are calculated to take cognizance of such offences, or to
investigate and reform the general polity of the state . . ." Doyle,
Impeachment Grounds, 5, citing *2 Wooddeson's Lectures*, Lecture 40,
596–97, 601 (1792 ed.) (emphasis added).

108. Regarding abuse of office and words used by James Madison ("Perfidy," and "schemes of peculation or oppression"), see note 22 above.
See charges against President Nixon and cases against President
Clinton; see cases of Judges Peck, Swayne, Archbald, English, Louderback, Ritter, Claiborne, Hastings, Nixon, Kent, and Porteous.

109. Regarding corruption and personal gain, see, for example, charges
against Judges English, Louderback and Ritter (abuse of power
to appoint and set the fees of bankruptcy receivers for personal
profit). See cases of Peck and English (vindictiveness, violation of
rights); see also cases of Judges Claiborne, Hastings, W. Nixon, and
Porteous.

See Judge Archbald's case, Charge 1, stating that the judge induced companies who were litigants to effect a sale so that he could
make a profit: "through the influence exercised by reason of his
position as such judge, willfully, unlawfully and corruptly did in-
duce" parties before him to conduct the transaction.

See Cole and Garvey generally, 14, and footnotes accompanying
text citing Staff of H. Comm. on the Judiciary, 93d Cong., *Constitutional Grounds for Presidential Impeachment* 20 (comm. print 1974);
VI *Cannon's* §§500–512; 514–524; 545–574; and *Impeachment of Alcee
L. Hastings*, H. Rep. 100-810, at 1–5 (1988); *House Practice* ch. 27 §4.

See also the cases of Judge Ritter; Judge Hastings; Judge Archbald; Judge English; and Judge Louderback for other abuses of office and financial improprieties. In addition to the wiretap disclosure allegations against Judge Hastings, see Bazan "Overview of Constitutional Provisions," 5, referencing introduction of 1993 H.R. Res. 177, 103rd Cong., to impeach Judge Robert P. Aguilar, indicted in 1989 and convicted of unlawful disclosure of a wiretap, with sentencing to prison, community service, and a fine. The conviction was reversed on appeal. After seven years of trials, retrials, and appeals, he resigned from office. No further action was taken on H.R. Res. 177, 103rd Cong. See the case of secretary of war William Belknap.

110. For example of abuse of office with obstruction of justice, coercion, intimidation, and sexual assault of employees, see the case of Judge Samuel Kent.

111. See H. Rep. 100-810 (1988), Impeachment of Alcee L. Hastings, Report of the Committee on the Judiciary to accompany H.R. Res. 499, 100th Cong., 6. See also case of Judge Samuel Kent, and H. Rep. 111-159 (2009), Impeachment of Judge Samuel B. Kent.

112. **Language in impeachment charge against President Nixon:**
- AGENCY: "using the powers of his high office, engaged personally through his subordinates and agents" in a course of conduct or plan designed to delay, impede and obstruct investigation; to cover up, conceal and protect those responsible to conceal the existence and scope of other unlawful, covert activities.

- RESPONSIBILITY FOR COVER-UPS OF SUBORDINATES: Knew or had reason to know that his close subordinates were impeding investigation into illegal activity and cover-ups, including those related to attorney-general confirmation, surveillance of citizens, break-in of the psychiatrist for Daniel Ellsberg, the leaker of the Pentagon Papers, and campaign financing practices of the Committee to Re-Elect the President.

Language in impeachment charge against President Clinton (originally numbered 3 in the House Proposal, this is Number 2 before the Senate): "Prevented, obstructed and impeded the administration of justice and, to that end, engaged personally, and through his subordinates and agents, in a course of conduct or scheme designed to delay, impede, cover up and conceal the existence of evidence and testimony related to a civil rights action brought against him in a duly instituted judicial proceeding."

Note the allegation of use of agents for whom the president would be liable.

Framers' intent: Framers James Madison and Abraham Baldwin both spoke to the president's responsibility and impeachment liability for his hires, and for his firing decisions, in debate in the First Congress.

James Iredell, later to become a Supreme Court justice, at North Carolina Ratifying Convention: The president "is of a very different nature from a monarch. He is to be . . . *personally responsible* for any abuse of the great trust reposed in him" (emphasis added). 1974 staff report, 9.

Responsibility of president as "Principal": "Col. Mason. No point is of more importance than that the right of impeachment should be continued. Shall any man be above Justice? Above all shall that man be above it, who can commit the most extensive injustice? When great crimes were committed he was for punishing the principal as well as the Coadjutors." Doyle, *Impeachment Grounds*, 9.

See also Hamilton, Federalist 70, "The Executive Department Further Considered," pars. 17–19, discussing the virtues of a single executive as opposed to the monarch of Great Britain, who can claim he was overruled by his council (par. 15). Hamilton argues the superiority of the American model, where the magistrate "ought to *be personally responsible for his behavior in office*, the reason which in the British Constitution dictates the propriety of a council not only ceases to apply, but turns against the institution" (par. 19, emphasis added). In Federalist 77, Hamilton emphasizes, with regard to the presidential liability for his appointments: "The blame of a bad nomination would fall upon the President singly and absolutely." Federalist 77, par. 5. Hamilton concludes in the final paragraph of that the President is "at all times liable to impeachment and trial . . ." Federalist 77, par. 11.

Use of agents for misconduct: See impeachment charges against Presidents Nixon and Clinton regarding use of agents, in Clinton pleading: acting "through his subordinates and agency": "Prevented, obstructed and impeded the administration of justice and, to that end, engaged personally, and through his subordinates and agents, in a course of conduct or scheme designed to delay, impede, cover-up and conceal the existence of evidence and testimony related to a civil rights action brought against him in a duly instituted judicial proceeding."

Use of agents for financial misconduct: See Secretary of War William Belknap who used intermediaries on both sides to obscure financial payoff, was impeached by the House, and resigned.

113. James Wilson, signer of both the Declaration of the Independence and the Constitution: "The executive power is better to be trusted when it has no screen. Sir, we have a responsibility in the person of our President; he cannot act improperly, and hide either his neg-

ligence or inattention; he cannot roll upon any other person his criminality; no appointment can take place without his nomination; and he is responsible for every nomination he makes . . . far from being above the laws, he is amenable to them in his private character as a citizen, and in his public character by *impeachment*" (emphasis in original). 1974 staff report, 9.

114. Regarding firing official "whose merits require he should be continued in the Office"; failure to choose successors or do the duties himself:

"Mr. Madison . . . The danger, then, consists merely in this—the President can displace from office a man whose merits require that he should be continued in it. What will be the motives which the President can feel for such abuse of his power, and the restraints that operate to prevent it? In the first place, he will be impeachable by this house, before the Senate, for such an act of maladministration; for I contend that the wanton removal of a meritorious officer would subject him to impeachment and removal from his own high trust," Doyle, *Impeachment Grounds*, 12.

The president had authority to remove subordinates, Madison reasoned, making "him, in a peculiar manner, responsible for the conduct" of executive officers. It would, Madison said, "subject him to impeachment himself, if he suffers them to perpetrate with impunity high crimes and misdemeanors against the United States, or neglects to superintend their conduct, so as to check their excesses." 1974 staff report, 15. Madison was supported by another framer, Abraham Baldwin of Georgia:

Mr. Baldwin: "If the President, 'in a fit of passion' removed 'all the good officers of government' and the Senate were unable to choose successors, the consequences would be that the President would be obligated to do the duties himself; or if he did not, we would impeach him, and turn him out of office, as he had others." 1974 staff report, 15.

115. See impeachment charges against Judges Porteous and Kent; Presidents Nixon and Clinton.

116. Regarding obstruction of justice: see impeachment charges against Judges Kent and Porteous; Presidents Nixon and Clinton.

117. Regarding conflicts of interest: "Incompatible Employment" in Doyle, *Impeachment Grounds*, 5, n. 5, quoting and discussing Wooddeson, who explained impeachments had been proper where a confidential advisor to the King had obtained "exorbitant grants or incompatible employment." The lectures by Wooddeson on English impeachment provide the foundation for much of the impeachment discussion in Jefferson's manual.

See also Federalist 73, par. 2, at the close of which Hamilton makes a clear statement of the purpose of emoluments prohibitions, and the importance of an independent president: "He can, of course, have no pecuniary inducement to renounce or desert the independence intended for him by the Constitution."

118. Regarding corruption and elections: George Mason of Virginia felt that "displacing an unfit magistrate" was "indispensable" in view of the "fallibility of those who choose, as well as by the corruptibility of the man chosen." Brown, 4. Later, at the Constitutional Convention, as it met as a Committee of the Whole on July 20, Mason adamantly defended the idea of impeachment, responding to an argument that reelection of the chief executive would be sufficient proof of his innocence:

"Col. Mason. No point is of more importance than that the right of impeachment should be continued. Shall any man be above Justice? Above all shall that man be above it, who can commit the most extensive injustice? When great crimes were committed he was for punishing the principal as well as the Coadjutors . . . One objection agst. Electors was the danger of their being corrupted by the Candidates: & this furnished a peculiar reason in favor of impeachments whilst in office. Shall the man who has practiced corruption & by that means procured his appointment in the first instance, be suffered to escape punishment, by repeating his guilt?" Brown, 4–5.

Morris at Constitutional Convention: "Mr.Govr. Morris's opinion had been changed by the arguments used in the discussion . . . The Executive ought therefore to be impeachable for treachery; Corrupting his electors, and incapacity were other causes of impeachment . . . This Magistrate [later named "President"] is not the King but the prime-Minister. The people are the King . . ." Doyle, *Impeachment Grounds*, 9.

Hamilton, too, feared for corruption. In his Federalist 68, "The Mode of Electing the President," he explained goals. "Nothing was more to be desired than that every practicable obstacle should be opposed to cabal, intrigue, and corruption. These most deadly adversaries of republican government might naturally have been expected to make their approaches from more than one quarter, but chiefly from the desire in foreign powers to gain an improper ascendant in our councils." Hamilton, Federalist 68, par. 5.

119. Regarding corrupt pattern of behavior, corrupt financial relationship, even prior to taking office and continuing in office: Readers should take care in citing Porteous as proof that impeachment may lie for misconduct preceding both nomination and service as a U.S. official. Judge Porteous's long-standing relationships with crooked

colleagues predated his federal position, but these wrongful acts were mixed in with the allegations of federal misconduct. Importantly, however, Porteous impeachment Article 4, an independent ground for conviction, focused on the judge's misconduct during his nomination process. The judge's lies, cover-up, and other misconduct gave rise to independent impeachment liability.

Judge Porteous's impeachment Article 1 alleged that Porteous, beginning as a state judge and while a federal judge, engaged in a corrupt pattern of conduct. As a federal judge he "engaged in a pattern of conduct incompatible with the trust and confidence placed in him" when he denied a motion to recuse himself in a case where he had a "corrupt financial relationship with the law firm representing one of the parties." Against canons of judicial ethics, Article 1 alleged, he failed to disclose that he had engaged in a corrupt scheme with two lawyers in that firm beginning while he was a state court judge in the late 1980s.

120. See Archbald (prior federal position misconduct) and Porteous (nomination misconduct) cases. Pre-federal nomination misconduct was not isolated as impeachable, or not in the Porteous impeachment articles.

121. See case of Judge Claiborne, impeached and convicted for providing false information on federal income tax forms, and President Clinton case, alleging cover-up of an affair, with the House managers making use of the Claiborne case as useful precedent; see Judge Porteous case involving bankruptcy fraud.

122. Regarding "Too ignorant to perform duties": Judge Lawrence defined misdemeanor as "bad conduct" and misdemeanor in England, without intent, as being too ignorant to perform duties, impeachable even if the official believed what he said. Lawrence, 648–650, 680, noting that the United States should construe the language equally with England. Lawrence, 644.

123. Judge Nixon was impeached for making false statements to the grand jury about whether he had discussed a criminal case with the prosecutor and attempted to influence the case, as well as for concealing such matters from federal investigators.

Regarding perjury and violation of court order: see Judge Porteous impeachment articles. Judge Porteous was charged and convicted under impeachment Article 3 for perjury in connection with the judge's personal bankruptcy filing, "and by repeatedly violating a court order in his bankruptcy case, thereby bringing his court into scandal and disrepute, prejudicing public respect for and confidence in the federal judiciary, and demonstrating that he is unfit for the office of federal judge." Article 3 then generally declared that the Judge was guilty of high crimes and misdemeanors and should be removed from office.

Regarding perjury and obstruction of justice: see case of Judge Sam Kent.

Regarding lying, perjury, and subornation of perjury: see Presidents Clinton and Nixon impeachment charges.

124. Regarding overreaching, abuse of authority, and self dealing, see discussion of Parliament's ability to deal with officials' "misconduct in office due to overreaching, abuse of authority, or self-dealing, each of which would constitute a high crime and misdemeanor . . . It was in this way that Quincy, Adams, and ultimately the framers of the Constitution understood the meaning of high crimes and misdemeanors by a public official and parliamentary usage." Brown, 26; see, for example, Judge Archbald impeachment.

125. Regarding depriving the public of "right to honest services of his office": Judge Porteous was charged, and convicted of making misleading statements in a recusal hearing, "depriving the higher court of critical information" for its review involving his denial of recusal, "depriving the parties and the public of the right to the honest services of his office."

126. Corruption of judicial process: See Clinton impeachment charges.

127. See Judge English impeachment Article 1 alleging that Judge English "did on divers and various occasions so abuse the powers of his high office that he is hereby charged with tyranny and oppression, whereby he has brought the administration of justice in [his] court . . . into disrepute, and . . . is guilty of misbehavior falling under the constitutional provision as ground for impeachment and removal from office." See Presidents Nixon and Clinton impeachment charges.

128. See impeachment of Judge Porteous. By virtue of "corrupt relationship" (Article 1) and his "corrupt conduct" (Article 2) as a federal judge, Judge Porteous was charged and convicted of having "brought his court into scandal and disrepute," having "prejudiced public respect for, and confidence in, the federal judiciary and demonstrated" that he was "unfit for the office of federal judge." Bazan, "Overview of Constitutional Provisions," 1.

129. Judge Claiborne, first convicted in a separate criminal proceeding, was impeached by the House for providing false information on federal income tax forms, the same basis as his criminal conviction. The Senate convicted on three of the four articles that described the judge's clearly wrongful conduct, as the House charged and proved to the Senate under Articles 1 and 2 that the Judge engaged in misbehavior and "high crimes and misdemeanors" war-

ranting removal for violations of federal law. Article 4 stated that the judge's actions brought the "judiciary into disrepute, thereby undermining public confidence in the integrity and impartiality of the administration of justice." The Senate convicted the judge on the Article 4 ground, as well as on Articles 1 and 2.

130. See President Clinton impeachment charges.

131. To Madison, it was "indispensable" that provision be made for "defending the Community agst [sic] the incapacity, negligence or perfidy of the chief magistrate." Doyle, *Impeachment Grounds*, 8.

132. Regarding revealing confidential information (wiretap): See Bazan, "Overview of Constitutional Provisions" 5, n. 24 referencing introduction of H.R. Res. 177, 103rd Cong., to impeach Judge Robert P. Aguilar; see impeachment of Judge Hastings: Article 16 alleged that, as supervising judge, Judge Hastings learned highly confidential information obtained through a wiretap and revealed highly confidential information that he learned as the supervising judge of the wiretap. "As a result of this improper disclosure, certain investigations then being conducted by law enforcement agents of the United States were thwarted and ultimately terminated." Article 17 was a catch-all provision, joining together all the other charges, also summarizing his judicial duties as including being "required to enforce and obey the Constitution and laws of the United States, to uphold the integrity of the judiciary, to avoid impropriety and the appearance of impropriety, and to perform the duties of his office impartially." His actions regarding the wiretap were said to "undermine confidence in the integrity and impartiality of the judiciary and betray the trust of the people of the United States, thereby bringing disrepute on the Federal courts and the administration of justice by the Federal courts." U.S. Senate website: https://www .senate.gov/artandhistory/history/common/briefing/Senate _Impeachment_Role.htm (accessed March 2017). See also H. Rep. No. 100-810 (1988), Impeachment of Alcee L. Hastings, Report of the Committee on the Judiciary to accompany H.R. Res. 499, 100th Cong.

133. See impeachment of Judge Kent; James Madison, on concerns warranting provisions for protecting the community from Executive Magistracy (later president): "He might divert his administration into a scheme of peculation or oppression. He might betray his trust to foreign powers." Brown, 6.

134. Resubverting the fundamental laws; introducing arbitrary power, supporting pernicious and dishonorable measures, see Wooddeson on English impeachment law, Doyle, *Impeachment Grounds*, 5.

135. Professor Arthur Hellman explained during House hearings con-

cerning the impeachment of Judge Samuel Kent that Judge Kent's conduct fit within two broad, overlapping impeachment categories: "serious abuses of power" and "conduct that demonstrates that an official is unworthy to fill the office that he holds." H.R. Rep 111–159, sess. of 2009, citing testimony of Professor Hellman, Sec. V.B.4.

136. See impeachment charges against Presidents Nixon and Clinton. See Pickering impeachment articles.

137. Regarding failure to provide Senate "every material intelligence he receives"; "giving false information to the Senate"; and "concealing important intelligence which he ought to have communicated:" James Iredell (later a Supreme Court justice), speaking at North Carolina Ratifying Convention about impeachment, said that the "President must certainly be punishable for giving false information to the Senate. He is to regulate all intercourse with foreign powers, and it is his duty to impart to the Senate every material intelligence he receives. If it should appear that he has not given them full information, but has concealed important intelligence which he ought to have communicated, and by that means induced them to enter into measures injurious to their country, and which they would not have consented to had the true state of things been disclosed to them, in this case, I ask whether, upon an impeachment for a misdemeanor upon such an account, the Senate would probably favor him." 1974 staff report, 14. In the Porteous impeachment case, Article 4, a separate ground for conviction, also explained that Judge Porteous's wrongdoing "deprived the United States Senate and the public of information that would have had a material impact on his confirmation."

138. Violating court order: Judge Porteous was charged and convicted under impeachment Article 3 for perjury in connection with his personal bankruptcy filing, "and by repeatedly violating a court order in his bankruptcy case, thereby bringing his court into scandal and disrepute, prejudicing public respect for and confidence in the federal judiciary, and demonstrating that he is unfit for the office of federal judge." Article 3 then generally declared that the judge was guilty of high crimes and misdemeanors and should be removed from office.

139. See Bazan, Elizabeth. *Summary of Impeachment Proceedings in the 111th Congress.* Congressional Research Service, April 2010 (electronic version in December 2010, updating her April 2010 book).

140. U.S. Senate website: https://www.senate.gov/artandhistory/history/common/briefing/Senate_Impeachment_Role.htm (accessed March 9, 2017); see also Bazan, *Overview of Constitutional Provisions*, providing details on the impeachment of Judge Samuel Kent and dismissal of his trial upon his resignation, and the impeachment and December 8,

2010 conviction of Judge G. Thomas Porteous, with disqualification from holding federal office.

141. Rehnquist, William, *Grand Inquests*, 27. Throughout *Grand Inquests*, the chief justice made clear his supreme respect for the U.S. constitutional system, the independence of the judiciary, the great idea of a presidential, not parliamentary. system of government, and the importance of the U.S. impeachment process as part of the constitutional framework.

142. Whitney, *Founders of Freedom . . . Constitution*, 55.

143. During the Revolution, Blount avoided fighting as his father arranged his job as paymaster, which he parlayed into the army's chief commissary agent, profiting greatly. He also drew his officer's salary, while serving himself as a merchant, investor, and land speculator. He served in state and federal legislatures in the 1780s, was a delegate to the Constitutional Convention in Philadelphia, and a signer of the U.S. Constitution, although he claimed his signature meant no approval, but rather merely showed that he was present. Whitney, *Founders of Freedom . . . Constitution*, 55–58.

144. Whitney, *Founders of Freedom . . . Constitution*, 55–59.

145. Whitney, *Founders of Freedom . . . Constitution*, 59.

146. See Morison, generally, 336–353. The tumultuous 1793–1796 time period saw the Barbary pirates enslaving American sailors, requiring rebuilding of the U.S. Navy, and the ransoming of the captured Americans in 1796. The United States found itself on the brink of war with England, as Britain declared any neutral ship sailing with provisions to the French West Indies a "good prize." Britain captured many American trading vessels in the Caribbean. As the British foreign minister exercised diplomacy to calm matters, President Washington sent Chief Justice John Jay to Great Britain. The goal: avoid war and accomplish British evacuation of Northwest American posts, all accomplished by Jay in a poorly received, but important treaty in late 1794. Ibid., 336–353. Washington also faced and successfully put down a tax rebellion of "moonshiners" in the "Whiskey Rebellion." The President made use of his pardon power in pacifying the rebel leaders, convicted of treason.

Washington managed multiple crises on multiple fronts. The United States Army battled Native Americans, including the Miami, the Shawnee, the Ottawa, Chippewa, Potawatomi, and Iroquois. The Battle of Fallen Timbers ended with Major General "Mad Anthony" Wayne's destruction of villages and building of Ft. Wayne, and a peace treaty in mid 1795, with Native American loss of lands, with promised enclaves for the tribes eventually lost to a wave of settlers, violating the Treaty of Greenville.

Washington also used diplomacy, sending Thomas Pinckney to Spain to successfully secure, in late 1795, rights of transit in New Orleans and navigation rights on the lower Mississippi. Spain left its posts on the east bank of the Mississippi, giving the U.S. control of its territory.

See Morison in general, and 343–45.

147. Morison, 343.

148. Whitney, *Founders of Freedom . . . Constitution*, 59.

149. The Blount impeachment articles charged the senator with high crimes and misdemeanors, conduct "contrary to the duty of his trust and station as a Senator, and against the peace and interests thereof" as follows:

Article 1 charged Blount with engaging in a military hostile operation "for the purpose of wresting" the Floridas and Louisiana, or parts thereof, from Spain, and of conquering the land for the king of Great Britain, in disregard of his duties and obligations of his high station as a U.S. senator, infringing and violating U.S. neutrality.

Articles 2 and 5 alleged that Blount conspired to incite the Creek and Cherokee nations to go to war against the Spanish subjects in the same lands, for the benefit of Great Britain; and foment discontent among the Cherokee nations against the United States.

Articles 3 and 4 charged Blount with interference with a temporary federal Indian agents' relationship and job functions with the Cherokee and Creek nations, in furtherance of his criminal designs. Simpson, Alex, *A Treatise on Federal Impeachments* (Philadelphia: Law Association of Philadelphia, 1916), Appendix, 191–92; see also Doyle, *Impeachment Grounds*, 16.

150. Whitney, *Founders of Freedom . . . Constitution*, 59; Brown,37.

151. Brown, 36–38, and n. 4–14.

152. Brown, 37–38.

153. Whitney, *Founders of Freedom . . . Constitution*, 60.

154. Ibid.

155. Brown, 38–39; regarding history of Blount's return and welcoming: Whitney, *Founders of Freedom . . . Constitution*, 60.

156. 1974 staff report, 42; Whitney, *Founders of Freedom . . . Constitution*, 60.

157. Whitney, *Founders of Freedom . . . Constitution*, 60.

158. Brown, 40, n. 29–31.

159. Judge Pickering was censured by his state legislature in 1794 due to erratic behavior and absences from the bench as chief of the New Hampshire Supreme Court, as his deteriorating condition became known as he was becoming a federal judge, with an appointment in 1795. Sadly, by 1803, Pickering was senile, habitually drunk, and

"a pathetic relic of a once honored and effective statesman." Brown, 40, n. 29–31.

Pickering in years past had been a respected advocate for ratification of the Constitution and a drafter of the New Hampshire State Constitution. By 1803, when the House authorized impeachment, no one contested the facts alleged: he was incapable of forming the legal intent to commit his wrongdoings; the judge's actions violated an Act of Congress; he refused to hear evidence from the U.S. Attorney; he refused to allow an appeal; and he gave away an entire, provisioned ship (seized by the Collector of Customs in the custody of the United States for non-payment) to the man who, while claiming ownership had no legal right to the vessel or cargo, having failed to prove any payment. Brown, 39–49; Simpson, 192–94.

160. Charge 1 summarized judicial misconduct of Judge Pickering in ordering a fully provisioned vessel with foreign merchandise to be delivered to a certain Eliphalet Ladd who produced no certificate of his claim, "contrary to his trust and duty as judge of the said district Clerk."

Charge 2 complained of Judge Pickering's refusal to hear the testimony of the U.S. Attorney's witnesses, ready to prove the forfeiture right of the United States to the vessel, as the Judge acted "with the intent to defeat the just claims of the United States," ordering the vessel restored to Eliphalet Ladd, "contrary to his trust and duty, as judge of the said district court."

Charge 3 described the judge's reaction to the U.S. appeal request "disregarding the authority of the laws, wickedly meaning and intending to injure the revenues of the United States, and thereby to impair their public credit, did absolutely and refuse to allow the said appeal . . . contrary to his trust and duty as judge."

Charge 4 described the need for faithful and impartial administration of justice, temperance, and sobriety in a judge, charging the judge with appearance on the bench "for administering justice, in a state of total intoxication, and did then frequently and in a most profane and indecent manner, invoke the name of the Supreme Being . . . and was then and there guilty of other high misdemeanors, disgraceful to his own character as a judge, and degrading to the honor and dignity of the United States." Simpson, Appendix, 193. See generally Simpson, Appendix, 192–94.

161. Founding Fathers Morris and Madison each spoke of incapacity as impeachment grounds. Doyle, *Impeachment Grounds*, 8–9, citing II FARRAND 64–9 (Madison) (July 20, 1787).

Pickering was regarded as "insane and infirm." Brown, 39–41 (Senate acknowledging Pickering's incapacity to serve as a judge).

See also Berger, 183–184 regarding evidence of Pickering's incapacity.

The son alleged his father's insanity made him "incapable of corruption of judgment," and much of the Senate's debate centered on whether Pickering's incapacity was sufficient grounds. Brown, 40. The Senate vote (19–7) convicted Pickering. Doyle, *Impeachment Grounds*, 17.

162. Decades later, eighteenth- to nineteenth-century writer Henry Adams, great-grandson of John Adams, called into question the Pickering case result, with political discord over judiciary appointments and removal issues, political anger over outgoing President Adams's last-minute appointments, and incoming Republicans supporting President Jefferson in efforts to control the judiciary. Brown, 41, n. 43, 46. Brown quotes Henry Adams disparaging any use of the matter as precedent, for trying an insane man who was not present and punished without counsel, and other irregularities. Brown, 41.

163. Hamilton boldly wrote that impeachable offenses "are of a nature which may with peculiar propriety be denominated POLITICAL, as they relate chiefly to injuries done to the society itself." Federalist 65, par. 2 (emphasis in original).

164. 1974 staff report, 26–27.

165. Per Berger, Henry Adams conceded that the insane man's lack of responsibility did not render the United States incapable of removing him "for the good of the public service." Berger, 184.

166. Berger certainly appears to agree that not only was Pickering's conviction the right result, it was consistent with the Founders' intent. Berger added additional compelling facts about Pickering's incapacity, offering further proof from Albert Beveridge's, *The Life of John Marshall* (Boston: Houghton Mifflin, 1916), 164–65, that Pickering "had been hopelessly insane for at least three years. . . and had become an incurable drunkard." Berger 183, n. 11 and accompanying text.

Berger agrees with Hamilton's assumption that insanity afforded ground for removal; and adds "I would venture that is was doubtless shared by the Framers; and it was buttressed by the centuries-old rule that a document should be construed to avoid an unreasonable or absurd result." Berger, 184.

For Madison on incapacity as grounds for impeachment, see note 22.

167. The Twenty-fifth Amendment does not eclipse congressional impeachment power. While the Constitution allowed for congressional law for "inability" both of the president and vice president per Art. II, Sec. 1, Clause 6, and the Twelfth Amendment, replaced by

the Twenty-fifth Amendment, there is nothing in the language or in the Twenty-fifth Amendment to the U.S. Constitution inconsistent with Congress using its powers of impeachment.

168. While an impeached officer could exercise his constitutional rights against self-incrimination, that right doesn't make the proceeding a criminal trial. The Constitution makes clear that the office-holder, independent of his or her impeachment trial, could still be liable for criminal indictment, trial, judgment, and punishment:

> Judgment in Cases of Impeachment shall not extend further than to removal from office, and disqualification to hold any Office of honor, Trust or Profit under the United States, but the Party convicted shall nevertheless be liable and subject to Indictment, Trial, Judgment and Punishment, according to Law. U.S. Constitution, Art. I, Sec. 3, Clause 7.

Alexander Hamilton, in Federalist 65, made it clear that the impeached offender could be further chastised separately from impeachment: "The punishment which may be the consequence of conviction upon impeachment is not to terminate the chastisement of the offender. After having been sentenced to permanent ostracism from the esteem and confidence and honors and emoluments of his country, he will still be liable to prosecution and punishment in the ordinary course of law." Federalist 65, par. 8.

169. The 1974 staff report noted that the crucial factor is not the intrinsic quality of behavior but the "significance of its effect upon our constitutional system or the functioning of government." 1974 staff report, 27. Pickering's removal from his high position as federal judge avoided future abuses.

170. Justice Chase, whose mother died during his birth, was raised and tutored with a classical education by his father, a professor from England before emigrating to America, and the rector of St. Paul's parish in Baltimore, Maryland. After admission to the bar and election to the colonial legislature, Chase battled the royal governor, instigated mob action against the Stamp Act and other British tyrannies, and, as a delegate to the First Continental Congress in 1774, was disappointed in his colleagues' efforts to find a peaceful solution. Whitney, David C., *Founders of Freedom in America: Lives of the Men Who Signed the Declaration of Independence* (Chicago: J. G. Ferguson, 1965), 63–64.

171. After the fighting began at Lexington and Concord, Chase spoke with force "shocking" to the Continental Congress delegates and won admiration for his "fearless exposure" of a fellow delegate to the 1775 Congress, who disclosed independence plans to the king's governor of Georgia. The Congress tasked Chase to recruit Ca-

nadians to join the rebellion, after which efforts he successfully roused the people of Maryland to change the voting directions of their delegation to support the Declaration of Independence, which Chase signed on August 2, 1776 after its approval on July 4. Whitney, *Founders of Freedom . . . Declaration of Independence*, 64–66.

172. Brown, 42; Whitney, *Founders of Freedom . . . Declaration of Independence*, 62–66.

173. See Rehnquist, 97–98.

174. See *Marbury v. Madison*, 5 U.S. 137 (1803), authored by Chief Justice John Marshall, who is also credited with developing the doctrine of "implied powers" inspired by George Washington's bold steps in signing the bill establishing the United States' first central bank, in an expansive view of the presidency. Chernow, 648–650. In the decision to sign the bill, President Washington turned to many for advice, then ultimately to Hamilton who "rose to the occasion as might be expected." Rehnquist, 38. Three decades later, Chief Justice Marshall upheld the constitutionality of the bank chartered by Congress, giving discretion to the legislature: "Let the end be legitimate, let it be within the scope of the Constitution, and all means which are appropriate, which are plainly adopted to that end, which are not prohibited, but consist with the letter and spirit of the Constitution, are Constitutional." Rehnquist, 38–39, citing *McCullough v. Maryland*, 17 U.S. 316 (1819). Regarding Chase's and Jefferson's actions, see Brown, 42, and Rehnquist, 90–104.

175. Grounds reproduced at Brown, App., pp. 135–39.

176. Brown, 43, n. 61.

177. See Brown, 42–43, n. 61–63.

178. Brown, 43.

179. Brown, 45.

180. For example, Chase took pains to ensure the defense counsel stayed on, and gave a light sentence. Rehnquist, 88.

181. Rehnquist, 89.

182. The first question boiled down to whether Chase had properly instructed the jury on the law. Chase had refused to hear argument on the definition of treason; Chief Justice Rehnquist in painstaking detailed analysis concluded in modern times, that, at most, it was an error of judgment, and surely not a ground for removal from office. The second and third charges—refusing to allow counsel to argue their view of the law to the jury—apparently weren't proved to the Senate. See Rehnquist, 58–73. The various remaining charges concerning the conduct of the Callender trial, on failing to properly apply Virginia law, failing to grant a continuance, and behaving in his rulings in a manner that would appear to dominate the pro-

ceedings, requiring, for example, that questions be put in writing or ridiculing defense counsel or insisting they abide by his earlier decisions or interrupting (albeit not in closing argument). Rehnquist acknowledged Chase's "overbearing" manner (Rehnquist, 85), but considering the law at the time found nothing so grave as to warrant impeachment. Rehnquist, 74–99. The law at the time—indeed until 1911—allowed, for example, for a judge to sit in a trial where he might have bias or favor; he was disqualified for *a financial interest* in the case, but no other disqualifications were permitted. Bias—the most controversial ground for disqualification—was rejected by the English common law practice entirely. Rehnquist, 87, n. 8. Berger took the position that Chase's charges were not trumped up and that he should have been convicted of the impeachment charges. See Berger, 224–251. Rehnquist strongly answered those allegations; indeed, he took a detailed half a book to do so. A point-by-point, fact-by-fact, detailed analysis by modern chief justice Rehnquist— applying the law at the time—demonstrates insufficient evidence or insufficient legal merit on many of these points, and painstakingly shows that the remaining attacks on Justice Chase's conduct to be unworthy of impeachment. Rehnquist, 15–105.

183. Rehnquist marshalled detailed evidence showing other judges' politicized speeches at the time of Chase. The differences between Chase's charge and the other judges' grand jury charges were political differences. Rehnquist offers multiple examples of other justices of Chase's vintage delivering politicized speeches no more partisan than the alleged words of Chase to the grand jury. Grand jury charges at the time evolved from "general reflections of the relative situations between the United States and France," "defense of the Alien and Sedition laws," "the present situation of the country," and "virtuous administration of government," to judges' charges that reflected "an increasing sense of apostolic mission." Rehnquist, 96–97.

184. Rehnquist, 94.

185. Rehnquist, 95.

186. Associate Supreme Court justice Joseph Story, who succeeded Justice Chase upon his death, described him with fondness. "His manners are coarse, and in appearance harsh, but in reality he abounds with good humor . . . In person, in manners, in unwieldly strength, in severity of reproof, in real tenderness of heart, and above all in intellect, he is the living . . . image of Samuel Johnson." Whitney, *Founders of Freedom . . . Declaration of Independence*, 67.

187. Chief Justice Rehnquist tells the story that the acquittal of Chase (of great importance to the future of an independent judiciary)

didn't prevent President Jefferson's continued sparring with the federal judiciary. When Aaron Burr's vice presidential term ended, Burr found himself in trouble and was indicted for treason for his alleged travel plans west of the Mississippi, via discussions with activists, to cause the secession of the southwestern states. President Jefferson took great interest in Burr's trial.

Justice John Marshall presided over the trial of Burr, who was acquitted, but held on a separate charge (a misdemeanor) of organizing an expedition against Spain. Such a charge, which was required to be brought in Ohio, never materialized. Marshall ruled against the U.S. government on a preliminary motion. Jefferson, displeased with yet another federal judge, wrote to Senate leader Giles of his wish that the Constitution be amended so as to correct the error "which makes any branch independent of the nation." Rehnquist, 117–118. Jefferson's annual message to Congress then suggested that "the legislature alone can apply or originate the remedy," referencing the outcome of the Burr trial. Congress didn't take the bait to pursue Marshall. Rehnquist, 118. Justice Chase had joined in Chief Justice Marshall's *Marbury v. Madison* opinion; the impeachment charges against Chase focused on his actions as a trial judge on circuit, not as an associate justice of the U.S. Supreme Court. Rehnquist, 115.

188. See Federalist 65 and 66, and note 57 above, for a summary of Hamilton's defense of the framers' choice of the Senate for the trial of impeachment. The Chase result is a case Chief Justice Rehnquist lauds, with the impeachment of President Andrew Johnson as one which "surely contributed as much to the maintenance of our tripartite federal system of government as any case decided by any court." Rehnquist, 278.

189. 1974 staff report, 46; Brown, 185, n. 77 (one may disregard Brown's typo at the top of page 46, indicating that Peck was convicted in the Senate; the error is set right in his superb note on page 185). The House Judiciary Committee recommended Peck's impeachment for his misconduct toward lawyer Lawless, as a high crime and misdemeanor involving "abuse of judicial authority" and "subversion of the liberty of the people."

190. Simpson, 197.

191. Brown, 185, n. 77.

192. 1974 staff report, 46.

193. Brown, 185, n. 77.

194. Humphreys and President Andrew Johnson, the Civil War–era impeachments, were prefaced by political shifts in the United States as the Founding Fathers departed the world, a world which experienced a growth in the abolition of slavery movement. With

the entry of Texas to the union in 1845 and acquisition of Oregon Territory, and Mexican cession, the country continued to make compromises over slavery, postponing but not solving the need for decision-making as to whether this country would continue to embrace the ownership of human beings. See Rehnquist, 150–211; Morison, 593–700.

195. See Rehnquist, 168; Morison, 592–93. "Flabby James Buchanan" ran against the Republican's promise of "Free soil, free speech, Fremont," but the only real issue was whether slavery would be permitted in the U.S. territories. Although Buchanan did well in the electoral vote, carrying every slave state except Maryland, he also carried Pennsylvania, Illinois, and Indiana, giving him 174 electoral votes to Fremont's 114 to Fillmore's 8. The Republican's "pathfinder" impressed with his 1.34 million votes to Buchanan's 1.838. The ominous numbers were seen in the source of Fremont's votes: all but 1,200 came from non–slave holding states. Morison, 593–700.

196. Morison, 593–700.

197. Alex Simpson, Jr., in his Appendix with Charges from English and American Impeachments, relied on the Congressional Globe, 2nd Session, 37th Congress, page 2,277 (1862) in reproducing the first line, which reads "Charge: High Crimes and Misdemeanors." The charges also allege that Judge Humphreys unlawfully conspired with Jefferson Davis and J. C. Ramsay to oppose by force the authority of the government of the United States (Charge 4) and unlawfully and in conjunction with other persons organize armed rebellion against the United States and levy war against them (Charge 3). He was convicted on all charges as high crimes and misdemeanors, with the exception of no conviction on 6(2) noted below.

Charges 1–7 accused Judge Humphreys of high crimes and misdemeanors. "Regardless of his duties" as a U.S. citizen and "unmindful of his duties" of his office, he publicly advocated secession, revolt, and rebellion; agreed to an act of secession; organized armed rebellion against the United States and levied war against them; conspired to oppose the United States; refused to hold court; acted as a judge for the Confederacy; and unlawfully arrested and imprisoned U.S. citizens. One of the Charges (No. 6) was split into three sections. Judge Humphreys was found guilty of all charges except 6(2) (confiscation of property of one Andrew Johnson and one John Catron). Simpson, Appendix, 197–99.

198. Catron was a U.S. Supreme Court Justice appointed by President Andrew Jackson.

199. Simpson, Appendix, 199.

200. ". . . this consideration [motive] was so unimportant that it was

never once mentioned on the trial . . ." Lawrence, 679–80.

201. See Simpson, Appendix, 197–99.

202. See 1974 staff report, 20, n. 92; see Simpson, Appendix, 197–199.

203. President Lincoln announced emancipation effective January 1, 1863, and was reelected in 1864 over McClellan, who garnered some votes in the hopes of a strong military showing. Northern victory came on April 9, 1865 at Appomattox, with General Grant ordering his troops to calm: "The war is over; the rebels are our countrymen again." See Morison, 593–700.

204. Rehnquist, 162–68.

205. Rehnquist, 168.

206. Morison, 740–41.

207. Morison, 711.

208. Morison, 712–13.

209. Rehnquist, 250.

210. Morison, 746.

211. Adversity and poverty in early life left Johnson—"essentially a Jacksonian Democrat"—with a chip on his shoulder, a vindictive and perverse temper, and great, "almost morbidly sensitive" pride. Rehnquist, 200, n. 1, 2; 205, 250–51.

212. Rehnquist, pp. 169–211.

213. Morison, 719–720; Rehnquist, pp. 250–51.

214. The Tenure of Office Act was finally repealed in the presidency of Grover Cleveland, at the executive's request, in 1887. Rehnquist, 261.

215. U.S. Senate website: https://www.senate.gov/artandhistory/history/common/briefing/Senate_Impeachment_Role.htm (accessed March 13, 2017).

216. Ibid.

217. Ibid.

218. Kennedy, John Fitzgerald. *Profiles in Courage.* (Illustrated edition) New York: Black Dog & Leventhal, 1998. Kennedy noted that the actual cause for which Johnson was tried "was not fundamental to the welfare of the nation," recognizing the absence of substantiality to the effect of Johnson's alleged maladministration; he also recognized the inadequacy of the "catch-all" clause, a conglomeration of all other articles (Art. 11), designed by Thaddeus Stevens in an attempt to furnish a common ground to convict. Kennedy also complimented President Johnson's "able counsel" in demonstrating that the Tenure of Office Act was null and void as unconstitutional, but even if it were valid, it would not apply to Secretary Stanton. *Profiles in Courage*, 144–46.

219. Chief Justice Rehnquist lists and analyzes the three "ablest and most respected" of the seven "Republican recusants" and their rea-

sons for acquittal. Rehnquist, 240–45. Each had valid, legal reasons for acquittal, including highly debatable application of the Tenure of Office Act (for which Johnson likely had the better interpretation); the unfairness to impeach a president of the United States for commenting freely on the conduct of other branches, and the importance of resisting the clamor of public opinion, and instead properly viewing the evidence. Radical Republicans such as Senator Sumner viewed impeachment, not as a trial, but as a vote of confidence under the British parliamentary system, and Johnson had stood in the way of the Reconstruction policies of the Republican Congress. Rehnquist, 245. Rehnquist analogized the attitude of Sumner to that of Senator William Giles, who, according to John Quincy Adams, said shortly before the Chase trial that he had tried to persuade another senator that impeachment meant "We want your office in order to give it to a better man." Rehnquist, 125.

220. The result from the President Johnson impeachment did not rely on some technical issue of failure to find criminal intent; apparently, a majority would not have required criminal intent to convict. During the trial, the debate raged as to whether the president must have some criminal intent, with a majority apparently deciding no criminal intent was required. Brown, 55–58. ". . . the criminal law limitation can fairly be said to have been rejected by a majority of the senators." Brown, 60–61. One senator also criticized the "catch-all" charge repeating certain articles (Art. 11); he found it hard "to ascertain what it really charges." Brown, 59. Strategies of test use, "catchall" and repetition are acknowledged in the U.S. Senate website: https://www.senate.gov/artandhistory/history/common/briefing/Senate_Impeachment_Role.htm (accessed March 13, 2017). The catchall became a recognized practice used historically in judicial impeachments, and passed muster, over objection, in the Ritter case.

221. Rehnquist, 245.

222. Rehnquist, 125.

223. 1974 staff report, 49.

224. 1974 staff report, p. 50; Belknap was not charged with bribery. Brown, 196, n. 1. Charges 1–5 alleged under "High Crimes and Misdemeanors in Office" financial improprieties by the secretary of war, who used his power and authority to appoint a person to maintain a trading post at Fort Sill, in order to receive personally or have paid to his wife, large sums of money, via an intermediary, from his appointee. Simpson, Appendix, 203–05.

225. The 1974 staff report explains that argument in the Senate included that the resignation prior to impeachment should cause the case to be dropped. The Senate decided to proceed, but twenty-two of the

senators voting "not guilty" on each article indicated that, in their view, the Senate had no jurisdiction. 1974 staff report, 50.

Simpson's massive Appendix to his *Treatise on Federal Impeachments* reports: "He was acquitted upon the ground that he had resigned his office as Secretary of War, and his resignation had been accepted by the President a couple of hours before the actual adoption of the articles of impeachment by the House." Simpson, Appendix, 203–05.

226. 1974 staff report, 20.

227. See generally 1974 staff report, 45–46, 50–53.

228. Simpson, Appendix, 207–13; see also Doyle, *Impeachment Grounds*, 18–19. Judge Archbald was removed from office and disqualified from holding any future office. 1974 staff report, 52, n. 5.

229. 1974 staff report, 51–52; Bazan, *Overview of Constitutional Provisions*, 27. See case of Judge Thomas Porteous for impeachment, which included a continuing pattern of misconduct dating back to nomination and, indeed, prior to federal service.

230. Bazan, *Overview of Constitutional Provisions*, 27–28. This CRS publication also lists several instances of allegations of prior misconduct in former capacities and their outcomes; Judge Porteous appears to be the first case where misconduct as a nominee for the federal position gave rise to independent impeachment liability and conviction.

231. Simpson, 213.

232. 1974 staff report, 53–54; Doyle, *Impeachment Grounds*, 23; House Comm. On the Judiciary, Constitutional Grounds for Impeachment Inquiry, 93d Cong., 2d sess. (1974), 50–54.

233. 1974 staff report, 20. Judge Ritter's misconduct also included income tax evasion, practicing law, and acceptance of gratuities, included as charges in a "catch-all" Article 7—the one article on which he was convicted. 1974 staff report, 55–57.

234. 1974 staff report, 55.

235. Rehnquist, 119.

236. Doyle, *Impeachment Grounds*, 20. Article 7 referenced the other six charges, the first two of which were dropped, but the fourth charge aggregated the other articles including income tax evasion, alleged in Articles 5 and 6 as "high misdemeanors in office" and willful failure to report or pay tax on income received by him. Ritter accepted, per the third charge, fees and gratuities from persons with large property interests within his territorial jurisdiction. The Senate convicted Judge Ritter on the one count re-incorporating articles. See also 1974 staff report, 20, 55–57.

The Chairman had overruled Ritter's complaint that his acquittal on the first six, specific charges rendered conviction on the "catch-all" clause improper, and found that the general charge number 7 was a separate charge. Ritter had been convicted on that sole charge. Ritter's attempt to attack the validity of the Senate proceedings in the Federal Court of Claims was dismissed on the broad "ground that no judicial court of the United States has authority to review the action of the Senate in an impeachment trial." 1974 staff report, 55–57 and n. 93, citing *Ritter v. United States*, 84 Ct. Cl. 293, 300, cert. denied, 300 U.S. 668 (1936).

237. Consider the early strategy in the case of Peck; the House decided to use only one, single article in the impeachment of Federal judge James H. Peck, stated the tenure provision of "good behavior" in addition to "high misdemeanors," and did not emphasize the substantial effect on society from the wrongdoing. The House emphasized the bad behavior of the judge but not the future risks he posed. The House voted to impeach in 1826 on a single article for Judge Peck's abuse of power in imprisoning and disbarring lawyer Mr. Lawless, who had publicly criticized the judge in a newspaper. The Peck charges included "subversion of the liberties of the people of the United States." The Senate acquitted Judge Peck on the one charge they were given.

238. In April 1952, when President Truman attempted to nationalize the country's steel mills, following unsuccessful negotiations with the United Steelworkers, Representatives in the House offered Resolutions to Impeach. Congress took no action on various resolutions, which included complaints regarding President Truman's firing of General Douglas MacArthur (in consultation with Generals Bradley and Marshall, plus respected civilian advisors, all of whom agreed that MacArthur must go for his declarations that war must be fought in Korea "for global supremacy"; Morison, 1071–1073), and for assigning U.S. armed forces to the United Nations command in Korea, as well as complaints of "attempting to disgrace the U.S., withholding information, and making reckless and inaccurate public statements." No committee action resulted. Stathis, Stephen, *Congressional Resolutions on Presidential Impeachment: A Historical Overview*, Congressional Research Service, September 16, 1998, 8–11. Representatives had filed Resolutions against Presidents Tyler, Andrew Johnson, Cleveland, and Hoover, as well as these Resolutions against President Truman, and the practice continues. Stathis summarizes instances in which Congress has considered proposals to impeach or to investigate the possibility of impeaching a president of the United States, citing the formal impeachment charges that have previously been brought against eight presidents

(Tyler, Andrew Johnson, Cleveland, Hoover, Truman, Nixon, Reagan, and Bush) leading up to the Resolutions against President Clinton, the first president impeached since Andrew Johnson.

239. Brown, 64–79. H. Lowell Brown provides a concise, readable, well-documented summary in *High Crimes and Misdemeanors in Presidential Impeachment*, 64–90. Leading authors involved in the matter provide firsthand knowledge and detail: Dash, Samuel, *Chief Counsel* (New York: Random House, 1976); Doyle, James, *Not Above the Law* (New York: William Morrow and Company, 1977); Sirica, John J., *To Set the Record Straight* (New York and London: W. W. Norton & Co., 1979); Dean, John, *Blind Ambition* (New York: Simon and Schuster, 1976).

240. Sirica, 299.

241. Rehnquist, 272.

242. Sirica wrote: "The grand jury's vote to name Nixon an unindicted co-conspirator tied the President to the cover-up and made the tapes germane to the proceedings." Sirica, 223. The president lost his fight to protect the tape recordings as the subpoena of the tapes was directly upheld without dissent by the Supreme Court, "the final demonstration that the judiciary was in fact a truly independent branch of our government." Sirica, 225–26; *United States v. Nixon*, 418 U.S. 683 (1974); see also Rehnquist, 272.

243. Sirica, 221–23.

244. The Senate Judiciary Committee developed key information on presidential wrongdoing from John Dean. Senate committee chief counsel Sam Dash describes his efforts to obtain Dean's story and to make the judgment as to whether to recommend immunity, a fascinating story of great lawyering. Dash, 97–125. Dash explains the difference between the methodical Watergate prosecution team and the Senate select committee. Senator Sam Ervin, chairman of the Senate select committee, explained how he regarded his duty: "When there is wrongdoing in the executive branch," the Senator said, citing Supreme Court authority, "it is the constitutional duty of the Congress to inform the public and provide remedial legislation." Dash, 124–25.

245. H.R. 803, 93rd Cong.; H. Rep. 93-1305 (1974).

246. These were the toughest Watergate sentences, except those given to the original Watergate burglars. Twenty-seven corporate executives pled guilty of providing dirty money to Nixon's 1972 reelection campaign. Doyle, *Not Above the Law*, 373–404.

247. Sirica, 301–02.

248. Sirica, 302.

249. Rehnquist, 74; 1974 staff report.

250. Brown 153–156; Cole and Garvey, 12, citing *Impeachment of Richard. M. Nixon*, H. Rep. 93-1305, at 1–4 (1974).

251. *Impeachment Grounds v. President Nixon*. The House Judiciary Committee considered five articles of impeachment against President Nixon. Three articles were referred by the House Committee on the Judiciary, but President Nixon resigned before they could be voted upon.

    1. Referred to House 27–11; 2. Referred to House 28–10; 3. Referred to House 21–17; Committee on the Judiciary, Debate on Articles of Impeachment Hearings Before the Committee on the Judiciary of the House of Representatives, 93d Cong., 2d sess. (1974); Brown, 63–90; Appendix 5, 153–56.

    Two other articles were considered, but not referred to the House, relating to (1) American bombing operations in Cambodia, false statements concerning those operations, disclosures resulting in illegal telephone interceptions, and creation of the "Plumbers Unit," formed initially in connection with Daniel Ellsberg's obtaining of the Pentagon Papers and their leakage; and (2) alleged benefits to the president at his homes from government expenditures and claims of improper and fraudulently claimed income tax deductions. Ibid.

252. 1974 staff report, 21.

253. 1974 staff report, 25–27.

254. "The decision of the judiciary committee to impeach Nixon for abusive but not criminal conduct is highly significant . . . The committee found in Nixon's conduct of the presidency the type of abuse and overreaching of presidential powers that threatened the constitutional order if left unremedied." Brown, 89. See generally Brown, 63–90; 1974 staff report.

255. Committee on the Judiciary, Debate on Articles of Impeachment Hearings Before the Committee on the Judiciary of the House of Representatives, 93d Cong., 2d sess. (1974); Brown, 63–90.

256. Dash, 265. The Senate Watergate committee—the Select Committee on Presidential Campaign Activities—was created by a 77–0 vote, and chaired by Senator Sam Ervin. The members were chosen with the goal of an objective, bipartisan investigation "that would have the confidence of the public." Dash, "Chief Counsel," 8–10. The Committee contributed much to the result in the Nixon impeachment investigation. Chief counsel for that committee, Sam Dash, explains his role, including his initial questioning of White House counsel John Dean and leading to discovery, via questioning of Alexander Butterfield, revealing that the president of the United States had taped many White House conversations.

See, for example, Dash, 55–175 regarding conversations with Dean and the phone call with an unhinged president; see 176–197 for stories of the tapes.

257. Dash, 265–66.

258. See Rehnquist, 119; Cole and Garvey, 12–13, *Impeachment of Judge Harry E. Claiborne*, H. Rep. 99-688, at 22–23 (1986); Impeachment of Judge Harry E. Claiborne, 132 CONG. REC. 29870-872 (1986); Doyle, *Impeachment Grounds*, 21.

259. See Cole and Garvey, 12–13, *Impeachment of Judge Harry E. Claiborne*, H.R Rep. 99–688, sess. of 1986, 22–23; Impeachment of Judge Harry E. Claiborne, 132 CONG. REC. 29870-872 (1986); Doyle, *Impeachment Grounds*, 21.

260. U.S. Senate website: https://www.senate.gov/artandhistory/history /common/briefing/Senate_Impeachment_Role.htm (accessed March 9, 2017).

261. See, for example, the Judge Kent case.

262. U.S. Senate website https://www.senate.gov/artandhistory/history /common/briefing/Senate_Impeachment_Role.htm(accessed March 9, 2017). See also H. Rep. 100-810 (1988), *Impeachment of Alcee L. Hastings*, Report of the Committee on the Judiciary to Accompany H.R. Res. 499, 100th Cong.

263. Bazan, *Overview of Constitutional Provisions*, 5, referencing introduction of H.R. Res. 177, 103rd Cong., to impeach Judge Robert P. Aguilar, indicted in 1989, and convicted of unlawful disclosure of a wiretap, with sentencing to prison, community service, and a fine. The criminal conviction was reversed on appeal. After seven years of trials, retrials, and appeals, he resigned from office. No further action was taken on H.R. Res. 177, 103rd Cong. Bazan, *Overview of Constitutional Provisions*, 5, n. 24.

264. U.S. Senate website: https://www.senate.gov/artandhistory/history /common/briefing/Senate_Impeachment_Role.htm(accessed March 2017). Impeachment of Judge Alcee L. Hastings Article 1 alleged that the judge "engaged in a corrupt conspiracy to obtain $150,000 from defendants" in a case tried before him, in return for the imposition of sentences which would not require incarceration of the defendants. He was convicted on Article 1.

Articles 2 through 15 listed and described alleged, specific perjurious actions concerning solicitation of bribe, making the deal to give probation for the bribe, nature of the bribe and the false versus true reasons he had meetings, coded conversations and telephone calls about the bribe and his motive. He was convicted on seven of these articles, involving lying and submitting false evidence in his criminal trial, which preceded his impeachment.

Article 16 alleged that, as supervising judge, Judge Hastings learned highly confidential information obtained through a wiretap and revealed highly confidential information that he learned as the supervising judge of the wiretap; Judge Hastings told the Mayor of Dade County, Florida, to stay away from a person known as "Waxy," who was "hot" and was using the mayor's name in Hialeah, Florida. "As a result of this improper disclosure, certain investigations then being conducted by law enforcement agents of the United States were thwarted and ultimately terminated." He was not convicted of this charge.

Article 17 was a "catch-all" (or aggregated or omnibus) provision, joining together the other charges, also summarizing the judge's judicial duties, including being "required to enforce and obey the Constitution and laws of the United States, to uphold the integrity of the judiciary, to avoid impropriety and the appearance of impropriety, and to perform the duties of his office impartially." The judge's misconduct served to "undermine confidence in the integrity and impartiality of the judiciary and betray the trust of the people of the United States, thereby bringing disrepute on the Federal courts and the administration of justice by the Federal courts." He was not convicted of this charge. See also H. Rep. 100-810 (1988), *Impeachment of Alcee L. Hastings*, Report of the Committee on the Judiciary to accompany H.R. Res. 499, 100th Cong.

265. *Nixon v. United States*, 506 U.S., 224, 226–7 (1993).

266. *Nixon v. United States*, 506 U.S., 226; see H. Rep. 101-36, at 13 (1989).

267. *Nixon v. United States*, 506 U.S., 224, 231 (1993). The chief justice added proof that the Founding Fathers' intent and words had not been altered by polishing work on the Constitution by the Committee of Style (which also polished the Impeachment Clause). Rehnquist explained that the Constitutional Convention's Committee of Style, in adding "sole," had no authority to alter the meaning of the clause, and captured what the framers meant, as a legal presumption. In fact, the chief justice continued, the Constitutional Convention voted on and accepted the Committee of Style's version that had polished the document.

268. *Nixon v. United States*, 506 U.S., 236. The impeachment charges against Judge Nixon alleged specific lies to a grand jury in a criminal matter, making the judge "guilty of an impeachable offense" for which "he should be removed from office." Judge Nixon was convicted on Articles 1 and 2. Judge Nixon's underlying conviction involved his ties to a businessman whose son benefited from the district attorney's dismissal of charges for drug smuggling. Judge Nixon tried to obtain a $150,000 bribe, and lied about it. Lewis, Neil

A. "Senate Convicts U.S. Judge, Removing Him from Bench," *The New York Times*, November 4, 1989.

Article 3 against Judge Nixon alleged the same underlying facts, raising "substantial doubt as to his judicial integrity, undermined confidence in the integrity and impartiality of the judiciary, betrayed the trust of the people of the United States and brought disrepute on the Federal Courts and administration of justice by the Federal Courts." There was no conviction on the general Article 3. Judge Nixon had been convicted in a criminal case for the perjury to the grand jury, then received the impeachment and conviction described above, in 1989, for his behavior, including making false statements to the grand jury about whether he had discussed a criminal case with the prosecutor and attempted to influence the case, as well as for concealing such matters from federal investigators.

Doyle, 22, citing Cong. Record 27101-104 (1989); Cole and Garvey, 14, citing *Impeachment of Walter L. Nixon, Jr.*, H. Rep. 101-136, at 1–2 (1989), and *House Practice*, ch. 27, §4.

269. *Nixon v. United States*, 506 U.S., 228. *Nixon v. United States* also had an immediate effect on the appeal of Judge Hastings. The Nixon decision compelled dismissal of Hastings' appeal, which had met with success at the trial court level. Bazan, 11–12.

270. Brown, 92.

271. Brown, 92–97. The court in the Paula Jones case ruled, after the president's deposition, that the Lewinsky relationship was not essential to the core of the Jones case. Brown, 96.

272. *The Washington Post* website: http://www.washingtonpost.com/wp-srv/politics/special/clinton/stories/mltestimony.htm (accessed July 4, 2017); Fernandez, 37.

273. Fernandez, 38.

274. Brown, 96.

275. Fernandez, 43.

276. Fernandez, 43–44; Brown, 97.

277. Brown, 97; Fernandez, 43; Office of Independent Counsel, Communication from Kenneth W Starr, Independent Counsel Transmitting a Referral to the U.S. House of Representatives in Conformity with the Requirements of Title 28, USC, Sec. 595c, Committee on the Judiciary, U.S. House of Representatives, 105th Congress, 2d Session, House document 105310 1998 U.S. Government Printing Office. See also Brown, 97; Fernandez, 43.

278. Brown, 100–101.

279. Brown, 108.

280. Brown, Appendix V1, 157–59, citing *Impeachment of William Jefferson Clinton*, H. Rep. 105-830, at 2, 4 (1988).

281. Fernandez, 99.

282. The Minority argued that, even if the misconduct (which focused on the president's lying under oath—perjury—and subornation of perjury, as he covered up an extra-marital affair) was a crime, it was not impeachable. The Minority report argued that, even if the criminal law violations were true, breaking the law to conceal a personal relationship did not amount to what they claimed was "an abuse of official power which is an historically rooted prerequisite for impeaching a President." See Bazan, *Overview of Constitutional Provisions*," 25 and accompanying footnotes. Breaking the law—or actions falling short of law-breaking—outside official duties, may be actionable in impeachment. See for example, Judges Clairborne, Nixon, Kent and Pickering cases.

283. The Majority staff report was adamant that the constitutional standard for impeachable offenses is the same for federal judges, as it is for all other civil officers, concluding that personal and professional misconduct may be involved and that impeachable offenses need not be federal or state crimes. The House rejected the Minority approach (regarding the lying, perjury issue as nonactionable personal misconduct), leading the way for future use of claims of "dishonesty" and violations of duty as measured by the particular responsibilities and duties of the job, against sitting presidents, enhanced by prior precedent from the Judge Claiborne and Judge Nixon cases (involving impeachment, perjury, and false statements unrelated to their official duties) that judicial cases were applicable.

    In the Clinton impeachment process, the House of Representatives and their impeachment managers made full use, in the Senate trial, of judicial impeachments, viewing those judicial impeachment activities as comparable, important, usable, and valid in evaluating the conduct of a president of the United States.

    "The House of Representatives impeached President Clinton for (1) providing perjurious and misleading testimony to a federal grand jury and (2) obstruction of justice in regards to a civil rights action against him. The House Judiciary Committee report that recommended articles of impeachment argued that perjury by the President was an impeachable offense, even if committed with regard to matters outside his official duties. The report rejected the notion that conduct such as perjury was 'more detrimental when committed by judges and therefore only impeachable when committed by judges.'

    "The report pointed to the impeachment of Judge Claiborne, who was impeached and convicted for falsifying his income tax returns—an act which 'betrayed the trust of the people of the

United States and reduced confidence in the integrity and impartiality of the judiciary.' While it is 'devastating' for the judiciary when judges are perceived as dishonest, the report argued, perjury by the President was 'just as devastating to our system of government.' In addition, the report continued, both Judge Claiborne and Judge Nixon were impeached and convicted for perjury and false statements in matters distinct from their official duties. Likewise, the report noted the President's perjurious conduct, though seemingly falling outside of his official duties, nonetheless constituted grounds for impeachment."

Cole and Garvey, 10–11, citing *Impeachment of William Jefferson Clinton*, H. Rep. 105-830, at 108, 110, 112, 113, 118, 119, and 132 (1988), Cong. Rec. S15, 760–62 (daily ed., October 9, 1986). "The Majority Staff endorsed the conclusion that the same constitutional standards should apply to both judicial and other civil officers, including the President." Brown, 104; see generally Committee on the Judiciary, Constitutional Grounds for Presidential Impeachment, Report of the Staff of the Impeachment Inquiry, U.S. House of Representatives, 105th Cong. 2d sess. (1998).

284. Cole and Garvey, 10–11, n. 81–84. citing *Impeachment of William Jefferson Clinton*, H.R Rep. 105–830, sess. of 1998, 108, 112, 113, 118, and 132 Cong. Rec. S15, 760–62 (daily ed., October. 9, 1986) (quotation marks omitted). House Impeachment Resolution with respect to William Jefferson Clinton H.R. 611, 105th Cong. Congress now has a long history of reliance on the 1974 staff report, post–Clinton impeachment, and its many key, controlling concepts, adopting the modern practice of use of judicial impeachment cases as precedent in a presidential impeachment.

285. Brown, 104–05, n. 89–90.

286. Ibid. "The House of Representatives impeached President Clinton for (1) providing perjurious and misleading testimony to a federal grand jury and (2) obstruction of justice in regard to a civil rights action against him. The House Judiciary Committee report that recommended articles of impeachment argued that perjury by the president was an impeachable offense, even if committed with regard to matters outside his official duties. The report rejected the notion that conduct such as perjury was "more detrimental when committed by judges and therefore only impeachable when committed by judges.

"The report pointed to the impeachment of Judge Claiborne, who was impeached and convicted for falsifying his income tax returns—an act that "betrayed the trust of the people of the United States and reduced confidence in the integrity and impartiality of the judiciary." While it is "devastating" for the judiciary when judges are perceived as dishonest, the report argued, perjury by the president was "just as devastating to our system of government." In addition, the report continued, both Judge Claiborne and Judge Nixon were impeached and convicted for perjury and false statements in matters distinct from their official duties. Likewise, the report noted the president's perjurious conduct, though seemingly falling outside of his official duties, nonetheless constituted grounds for impeachment."

Cole and Garvey, 10–11, citing *Impeachment of William Jefferson Clinton*, H. Rep. 105-830, at 108–19 and 132 (1998), Cong. Rec. S15, 760-62 (daily ed. October 9, 1986) (quotation marks omitted).

Impeachment covers much more than large-scale abuses commensurate with the intent and heavy evidentiary proof requirements of treason and bribery, as the history of American impeachment demonstrates in practice, as well as in the storied history of the colonists incorporating British impeachment concepts.

The concept of high Crimes and Misdemeanors encompasses a wide variety of conduct because the focus is on the harm caused by a public official, and not the person's intent; even great treachery and clear bribe-taking cases (Confederacy judge West Humphreys and appointer-of-friend-to-lucrative-position-for-big-bucks Secretary of War Belknap) are not charged as such in U.S. impeachments. Congress wisely choses to consider the offenses as belonging to "high Crimes and Misdemeanors."

Certainly many people argue whether the Clinton facts supported an impeachment charge, for example, whether the lies involved were "material" so as to even rise to the level of "perjury" in ordinary, prosecutorial discretion; but perjury—and other forms of personal and official misconduct—have indeed served as a legal basis for impeachments other than that of president Clinton. The key factor is not the claimed offense or intent; rather, the harm to society is the paramount consideration.

287. Ibid. H.R. 611, 106th Cong.
288. The words "manifest injury" did appear in the impeachment articles against President Clinton.
289. Brown, 102.
290. Alexander Hamilton wrote of division of power between the House, holding the power to "accuse," and the Senate with power to judge the case. He justified and explained his faith in Congress and why the framers of the Constitution placed all impeachment powers in Congress; he believed the House and Senate best suited for impeachment responsibilities.

For defending the use of a legislative body for divided rights of accusing to the House and judging to the Senate, see Federalist 66, par. 2. In Federalist 66, Hamilton continues to acknowledge the objection that this division places much power in the Senate, but finds the objection too imprecise; and he continues his justifications for his confidence in the Senate, emphasizing the duration of senators' terms, and the balance of other powers into the House; for example, the House has exclusive power for origination of money bills and the sole power to institute impeachment. Federalist 66, pars. 4–7. In Federalist 65, par. 7, he previously recognized the "awful discretion" lying with the Senate in impeachment, which forbids trusting impeachment power to a "small number of persons."

As with many cases, particularly those of Judge Peck, Justice Chase, and President Johnson, the ultimate responsibility fell to the Senate, where the question would necessarily involve substantiality of effect on society of the charges; in certain cases, the impact is insufficient and the Senate can choose, by acquittal, not to exercise their power to remove.

291. Fernandez, 78. This House approach, in retrospect, seems akin to an apology for not considering the key factor of "substantiality" of effect, as expressed in the 1974 staff report. Yet, the House willingness to impeach, and thereby overlook the lack of substantial effect of President Clinton's conduct was countered by the end result by the Senate, where the vote never came close to two-thirds. This is the result predicted by Alexander Hamilton in his writings, in Federalist 65, describing a divided process, and Federalist 66 explaining the House possesses the "the right of accusing" while lauding the ability of the Senate to come to a more deliberative solution than the House or any other body. In Federalist 65, paragraphs 8 and 9, Hamilton addresses the reasoning for not utilizing the Supreme Court, or some other entity, for the trial, while still obtaining the benefits of union with the Supreme Court by using the chief justice of the Supreme Court to preside over the court of impeachment. The Senate, clearly, holds the right of judging and the House holds the right to accuse. Federalist 66, par. 2.

292. Brown, 107.

293. Procedurally, members of the president's party (Democrats) on the House Judiciary Committee had argued against prolonged hearings, but political results intervened, as the Democrats gained five House seats in the November 3, 1998 elections. The tables turned and Republicans urged a faster process; the Republican Chairman Hyde committed to end hearings by the end of 1998, preventing any material witnesses from testifying and causing use of eighty-one written questions to the president. Fernandez, 76–77.

294. Fernandez, 76–77.

295. House managers began with a fact presentation on January 15, 1999, and closed with arguments on January 16, followed by the president's counsel presenting defense and closing statements.

   Senators used written questions to the parties in a question-and-answer session. The Senate voted to make the deliberations closed to the public. On January 27, 1999, the Senate voted 56–44 to not dismiss charges; therefore, the trial went on. The number of witnesses was limited, and witnesses did not appear live but rather by video depositions. See generally Fernandez, 85–97.

296. Kent eventually confessed to the assaults in connection with his plea to obstruction of justice, having lied and falsely claimed that any sexual activity was consensual. House report-recommended articles of impeachment alleged and marshalled proof that, between 2003 and 2007, then-Judge Kent repeatedly sexually assaulted his employees and then repeatedly lied about his conduct after the women reported it (to the Fifth Circuit, the FBI agents investigating, and the Department of Justice). See H. Rep. 111-159 (2009), H.R. 520, 111th Cong.

297. H. Rep. 111-159 (2009)—Impeachment of Judge Samuel B. Kent: www.gpo.gov/fdsys/pkg/CRPT-111hrpt159/html/CRPT-111hrpt159.htm.

298. H. Rep. 111-159, at sec. IV (2009) citing Transcript of Sentencing, *United States v. Kent* (U.S. So. Dist. Tex. Houston Div.), May 11, 2009.

299. Ibid. at note 14. Transcript of Sentencing, *United States v. Kent*, Crim. No. 4:08CR0596-RV (U.S. So. Dist. Tex., Houston Div.), May 11, 2009.

300. At sentencing, the prosecutor explained that Judge Kent didn't just lie, he confessed to one of the victims that he had denied her allegations and sent a clear message to his victim that she must also repeat the lie. H.Rep 111-159 (June 17, 2009), sec. IV, n. 9. Citing Transcript of Sentencing, *United States v. Kent* (U.S. So. Dist. Tex. Houston Div.), May 11, 2009.

301. H. Rep. 111-159, at sec. IV.B, n. 7 (2009), Order of Reprimand and Reasons, in re Complaint of Judicial Misconduct against U.S. D. Judge Samuel B. Kent, Judicial Council of the Fifth Circuit, September 28, 2007.

302. Kent asked for meetings with the FBI and other law enforcement and lied to them in December 2007. Prior to the first indictment in August 2008, Judge Kent, through his lawyers, asked for and received a meeting with major players at Main Justice Headquarters. Kent proceeded to lie to the trial team, to the FBI agents present, to the chief of the Public Integrity Section, and to the acting assistant attorney general. For example, then-Judge Kent said that any attempt to

characterize his conduct with the deputy clerk as nonconsensual was "absolutely nonsense." H. Rep. 111-159, at sec. IV.B (2009).

303. H. Rep. 111-159, at sec. IV.D. and E. (2009), citing Transcript of Sentencing, *United States v. Kent* (U.S. So. Dist. Tex. Houston Div.), May 11, 2009. Regarding procedural history, Kent's sentencing and the Fifth Circuit's recommendation of impeachment following conviction, see Bazan, *Overview of Constitutional Provisions*, 5–6, n. 25–31.

304. H.R. Rep 111–59, sess. of 2009, sec. IV.E.

305. Paschenko, Chris, "U.S. House approves Kent Impeachment." *Houston Chronicle*, June 20, 2009; Bazan, *Overview of Constitutional Provisions*, 5–6. See also H.R. 520, 111th Cong.

306. See generally Bazan, *Overview of Constitutional Provisions*, 5–6; H.R. 520, 111th Cong.; H.R. Rep 111–159, sess. of 2009 at V.E.; on May 12, 2009, Congressmen John Conyers, Jr., and James Sensenbrenner introduced Impeachment Resolutions, H.R. Res. 424, 111th Cong, and H.R. Res. 431, 111th Cong.

307. The House Task Force took expert testimony from Professor Arthur D. Hellman on the origin of "high Crimes and Misdemeanors," and the importance of English law Historian Richard Wooddeson. Hellman explained that Judge Kent's conduct fit within two broad, overlapping impeachment categories: "serious abuses of power" and "conduct that demonstrates that an official is unworthy to fill the office that he holds." H. Rep. 111-159, at sec. V.B.4 (2009).

308. Witness testimony provided more details of assaults, including the last sexual assault on March 23, 2007, where the witness said she left in tears, was asked by a security officer if Judge Kent had "tried to hit on me," and indicated "yes." H.R. Rep 111-159, at sec. V.B. (2009).

309. H. Rep. 111-159, at V.B. (2009).

310. Ibid.

311. The Congressional Research Service cites the Congressional Record in stating that the House agreed to each of the four articles of impeachment, by unanimous consent, in separate votes. Bazan, *Summary of Impeachment*, 4, n. 15, citing 155 Cong. Rec. H7066-7067 (daily ed., June 19, 2009). See also H. Rep. 111-159 (2009)—Impeachment of Judge Samuel B. Kent: www.gpo.gov/fdsys/pkg/CRPT-111hrpt159/html/CRPT-111hrpt159.htm.

An interesting historical footnote to the Kent impeachment involves former Judge Hastings, removed from office by impeachment but not barred from future office-holding. Alcee Hastings, elected to the U.S. Congress, sat in the House during the impeachment of Judge Samuel Kent. Gamboa, Susan, "House Impeaches Federal Judge from Texas," *Houston Chronicle*, June 19, 2009.

312. See H.R. 520, 111th Cong., and Bazan, *Summary of Impeachment*, 4–5.

313. Olsen, Lise, "Judge Kent resigns amid impeachment proceeding," *Houston Chronicle*, June 25, 2009; Paschenko, *Houston Chronicle*, June 20, 2009; Gamboa, Susan, "House Impeaches Federal Judge from Texas," *Houston Chronicle*, June 19, 2009. Judge Kent handed a " letter of resignation, effective June 30, 2009, to Senate officials who served a summons on him to appear in connection with ongoing Congressional impeachment proceedings. The Senate agreed to the dismissal of the articles of impeachment against former Judge Kent on July 22, 2009. Bazan, *Overview of Constitutional Provisions*, 6. Congressman Jim Sensenbrenner, R-Wisconsin, who served as one of the House managers, spoke to the *Houston Chronicle* of the resignation letter: "Kent's realization that we would not allow him to take advantage of the system proves that the system works and justice has been served. I hope the process reminds other judges that they are not above the laws they took an oath to uphold. I hope the women Mr. Kent assaulted will find some closure that he is behind bars and no longer being able to serve on the bench or collect a taxpayer funded paycheck. Olsen, *Houston Chronicle*, June 25, 2009. See also H. Rep. 111-159, at 111 (2009)

314. *Nixon v. United States*, 506 U.S., 224 (1993).

315. See H. R.Rep. 111-159 (2009), H.R. 520, 111th Cong. See Bazan, *Overview of Constitutional Provisions*, 5–6 for much procedural detail on Judge Kent; Tennissen, Marilyn, "Fifth Circuit Denies Kent's Disability Status, Recommends Impeachment," *Southeast Texas Record*, May 28, 2009; Witherspoon, Tommy, "Rep. Flores: Judge's Punishment Did Not Fit the Crime," *Waco Tribune-Herald*, January 22, 2016 (referring to sexual assaults by U.S. District Judge Walter S. Smith, reprimanded, and Rep. Bill Flores's intentions to explore impeachment of Judge Smith; Olsen, *Houston Chronicle*, June 25, 2009; Paschenko, *Houston Chronicle*, June 20, 2009; Gamboa, *Houston Chronicle*, June 19, 2009.

The House impeachment was by no means based on the criminal conviction. H. Rep. 111-159 (2009). The House performed its own investigation, and cited devastating statements from the victims, contained within H. Rep. 111-159 (2009), as, for example, a June 2009 victim statement specifically describing sexual assaults and the judge's response that even security who might hear would do nothing, since everyone feared the judge. Three of the four articles received unanimous consent; the fourth was unanimous with the exception of one "present."

The lead House manager, Adam Schiff, D-California, said, "Judge Kent's conduct undermined the institution of the judiciary and the public's confidence . . . Regrettably, impeachment was necessary to secure his removal from office, but I believe his resignation, when accepted will obviate the need to put his victims through any further ordeal." Olsen, *Houston Chronicle*, June 25, 2009.

316. H. Rep. 111-159 (2009).

317. H.R. 520, 111th Cong. (citing H. Rep. 101-36 (1989), Impeachment of Walter L. Nixon Jr. Report of the Committee on the Judiciary to Accompany H.R. Res. 87, 101st Cong,), p. 5; and H. Rep. No. 100-810 (1988), Impeachment of Alcee L. Hastings, Report of the Committee on the Judiciary to accompany H.R. 499, 100th Cong., 6. The "Brief Discussion of Impeachment" then concluded by reemphasizing, again recognizing the criminal nature of Judge Kent's misconduct, that ". . . the principles that underpin the propriety of impeachment do not require the conduct of issue be criminal in nature, or that there have been a criminal prosecution." Ibid.

318. Article 1:

- Alleged that Judge Porteous, beginning as a state judge and while a federal judge, engaged in a corrupt pattern of conduct. As a federal judge he "engaged in a pattern of conduct incompatible with the trust and confidence placed in him" when he denied a motion to recuse himself in a case where he had a "corrupt financial relationship with the law firm representing one of the parties." Against canons of judicial ethics, the article alleged, he failed to disclose that he had engaged in a corrupt scheme with two lawyers in that firm beginning while he was a state court judge in the late 1980s.

- Alleged the judge made misleading statements in the recusal hearing, "depriving the higher court of critical information" for its review involving Judge Porteous's denial of recusal, "depriving the parties and the public of the right to the honest services of his office."

- Alleged he solicited and accepted things of value from those attorneys while the case was pending before him, and, without disclosing this, ruled in favor of those attorneys' client.

- By virtue of the "corrupt relationship" and his conduct as a federal judge, Judge Porteous

- Brought his court" into scandal and disrepute,

- Prejudiced public respect for, and confidence in, the federal judiciary, and

- Demonstrated that he was unfit for the office of federal judge.

For this conduct, Article 1 then declared that Judge Porteous was "guilty of high crimes and misdemeanors and should be removed from office."

Article 2:

- Alleged the judge, both as a state court judge and as a federal judge, engaged in a "longstanding pattern of corrupt conduct that demonstrates his unfitness to serve as a U.S. district court judge, by engaging in a corrupt relationship with a bail bondsman and his sister, soliciting and accepting numerous things of value from them while taking official actions that benefitted them and using the power and prestige of his office to assist their business."
- Alleged the judge knew the bail bondsman made false statements to the FBI in an effort to assist the judge in being appointed to the federal bench.

Article 2 then generally declared that the judge engaged in conduct so utterly lacking in honesty and integrity that he is guilty of high crimes and misdemeanors, is unfit to hold the office of federal judge, and should be removed from office.

Article 3 alleged perjury in connection with the judge's personal bankruptcy filing, "and by repeatedly violating a court order in his bankruptcy case, thereby bringing his court into scandal and disrepute, prejudicing public respect for and confidence in the federal judiciary, and demonstrating that he is unfit for the office of federal judge."

Article 3 then generally declared that the judge was guilty of high crimes and misdemeanors and should be removed from office.

Article 4 alleged that:

- Prior to his appointment, and in connection with his nomination to be a U.S. district court judge, Judge Porteous "knowingly made material false statements about his past to both the United States Senate and to the FBI" in order to obtain his office;
- Failed to disclose the corrupt relationships with the law firm and the bail bondsman described in the first two articles or to disclose his knowledge that such bail bondsman had given false statements to the FBI in an effort to assist the judge in being appointed to the federal bench;
- Deprived the United States Senate and the public of information that would have had a material impact on his confirmation.

Article 4 then generally declared that the judge was guilty of high crimes and misdemeanors and should be removed from office.

Bazan, *Overview of Constitutional Provisions*, 1–2, n. 1–2. Judge Porteous was convicted on all four of the quoted articles, covering the described variety of financial, corruption, and other abuses.

319. Bazan, *Overview of Constitutional Provisions*," 2–6, 27–28.
320. See Bazan, *Summary of Impeachment*, 28; n. 1–3; Bazan, *Overview of Constitutional Provisions*, 1–6. The impeachment investigation

of Judge Porteous began in 2008; he was impeached on March 11, 2010, and he was convicted on December 8, 2010 on each of the four articles of impeachment. The vote on Article 1: 96–0; on Article 2: 69–27; on Article 3: 88–8; and on Article 4: 90–6. He was therefore removed from office and in an unusual additional judgment (94–2), the Senate voted to disqualify Judge Porteous from holding any future federal office. Porteous therefore joined two other judges impeached in the House and convicted in the Senate (and therefore removed from office) and also disqualified by separate Senate vote from holding any future federal office. Bazan, *Overview of Constitutional Provisions*, 5.

321. The Congressional Research Service explains:

"Judge G. Thomas Porteous was the first person to have been impeached by the House and convicted by the Senate based, in part, upon conduct occurring before he began his tenure in his federal office . . . The allegations in article IV involve entirely pre-federal conduct, albeit conduct directly related to his appointment to the federal bench. Article III alleged personal misconduct in connection with his Chapter 13 bankruptcy case." Bazan, *Overview of Constitutional Provisions*, 28.

322. In addition to convicting Porteous, the Senate voted 94–2 to disqualify him from holding any future federal office. Porteous therefore joined two other impeached, convicted Judges (Humphreys and Archbald) removed from office, who were also disqualified by separate Senate vote from holding future federal office. See Bazan, *Overview of Constitutional Provisions*, 5, 28.

323. Chief Justice Rehnquist recognized that the preparation and spotlight of the Nixon Watergate impeachment produced "much reasoned discussion, both within and without the [Judiciary] Committee, as to the nature of Impeachment." Rehnquist, 274.

324. Chief Justice Rehnquist prefaced his history book on impeachments by quoting the Constitution's Impeachment Clause, including "other high Crimes and Misdemeanors," noting:

"The framers were sufficiently practical to know that no charter of government could possibly anticipate every future contingency, and they therefore left considerable room for 'play in the joints.' Nor did they try to foresee exactly how each of the many powers and checks and balances they conferred and established would work out in particular situations. That was of necessity left to future generations." Rehnquist,10.

325. Simpson, 192–94; Brown, 39–41, including 40 acknowledging Pickering's incapacity to serve as a judge; Berger, 183–84 regarding evidence of Pickering's incapacity. The concept of injury to the United

States—regardless of intent or crime—as the main factor for impeachability was demonstrated in the first impeachment conviction: Judge Pickering's for conduct "degrading to the honor and dignity of the United States." See charges against Judge Pickering for "high Crimes and Misdemeanors," and accounts of the conduct of the trial; the House pled both intentional acts—unprovable in this case—as well as "other high misdemeanors . . . degrading to the honor and dignity of the United States." Simpson, 192–94. The Senate convicted Judge Pickering.

The Clinton presidential impeachment also pled injury to the United States in charging "high Crimes and Misdemeanors": The Clinton impeachment included allegations that the president "has undermined the integrity of his office, has brought disrepute on the Presidency, has betrayed his trust as President, and has acted in a manner subversive of the rule of law and justice, to the manifest injury of the people of the United States." Impeachment of William Jefferson Clinton, H. Rep. 105-830, at 2,4 (1998). The Senate acquitted President Clinton.

BIBLIOGRAPHY

Alden, John. *George Washington: A Biography.* New York and Avenel: Wings Books, 1984.

Bazan, Elizabeth. *Summary of Impeachment Proceedings in the 111th Congress* (CRS Report No. 7-5700 98-186). Washington, DC: Congressional Research Service,2010.

Bazan, Elizabeth. *Impeachment: an Overview of Constitutional Provisions, Procedure, and Practice* (CRS Report No. 7-5700 98-186). Washington, DC: Congressional Research Service, 2010.

Berger, Raoul. *Impeachment: The Constitutional Problems.* Cambridge: Harvard University Press, 1973.

Black, Charles. *Impeachment: A Handbook.* New Haven and London: Yale University Press, 1974.

Blackstone, William. *Commentaries on the Laws of England.* Clarendon Press at Oxford, 1765–1769.

Brown, H. Lowell. *High Crimes and Misdemeanors in Presidential Impeachment.* New York: Palgrave Macmillan, 2010.

Caird, Jack Simpson. "Impeachment." Briefing Paper Number CBP7612. House of Commons Library (June 6, 2016). http://researchbriefings .files.parliament.uk/documents/CBP-7612/CBP-7612.pdf.

Chernow, Ronald. *Washington: A Life.* New York: Penguin, 2010.

Cole, Jared and Todd Garvey. Impeachment: Grounds for Removal (CRS Report: 7-5700 R44260). Washington, DC: Congressional Research Service, 2015, https://fas.org/sgp/crs/misc/R44260.pdf.

Congressional Research Service, "Conflicts of Interest and Presidency." CRS Legal Sidebar, Oct. 14, 2016. https://fas.org/sgp/crs/misc /conflicts.pdf.

Dash, Samuel. *Chief Counsel.* New York: Random House, 1976.

Dean, John. *Blind Ambition.* New York: Simon and Schuster, 1976.

Doyle, Charles. *Impeachment Grounds: A Collection of Selected Materials* (CRS Report). Washington, DC: Congressional Research Service, updated 1998, https://www.senate.gov/CRSpubs/dfe6ac8e-78ad-4e59-bcda-d612c382ec2f.pdf.

Doyle, James. *Not Above the Law.* New York: William Morrow and Company, 1977.

Ellis, Joseph. *His Excellency: George Washington.* New York: Alfred A. Knopf, 2004.

Fernandez, Justin. *High Crimes and Misdemeanors: The Impeachment Process.* Philadelphia: Chelsea House Publishers, 2001.

Freedman, Eric M. "On Protecting Accountability." 27 *Hofstra Law Review*: Iss. 4, Article 3 (1999): http://scholarlycommons.law.hofstra.edu/hlr/vol27/iss4/3.

Gamboa, Susan. "House Impeaches Federal Judge from Texas," *Houston Chronicle*, June 19, 2009.

Glassman, Matthew E. *Separation of Powers: An Overview* (CRS Report 7-5700 R44334). Washington, DC: Congressional Research Service, 2016, https://fas.org/sgp/crs/misc/R44334.pdf.

The Great Impeachment and Trial of Andrew Johnson, with the Whole of the Preliminary Proceedings in the House of Representatives and the Senate and the Whole of the Proceedings in the Court of Impeachment, with the Decisions of Chief Justice Chase, and the Verdict of the Court. Philadelphia: T. B. Peterson & Brothers, 1868; reproduced by Forgotten Books, 2015.

Hamilton, Alexander, James Madison, and John Jay. *The Federalist Papers.* Mineola: Dover Publications, 2014.

Howe, Daniel Walker. *What Hath God Wrought: The Transformation of America, 1815–1848.* New York: Oxford University Press, 2007.

Hutton, R. *The Making of the Secret Treaty of Dover 1668–1670.* New York: Cambridge University Press, 1986: http://www.jstor.org/stable/2639064 (abstract accessed May 14, 2017).

Kennedy, David M. *Freedom from Fear: The American People in Depression and War, 1929–1945.* New York: Oxford University Press, 1999.

Kennedy, John Fitzgerald. *Profiles in Courage.* (Illustrated edition.) New York: Black Dog & Leventhal, 1998.

Lawrence, William. "The Law of Impeachment," 6 American Law Register (1867), p. 641–680, reprinted by University of Pennsylvania Law Review.

Lewis, Neil A., "Senate Convicts U.S. Judge, Removing Him from Bench." *The New York Times*, Nov. 1989.

Maskell, Jack. *Financial Assets and Conflict of Interest Regulation in the Executive Branch* (CRS Report 7-5700 R43365). Washington, DC: Congressional Research Service, updated 2014, https://fas.org/sgp/crs/misc/conflicts.pdf.

Morison, Samuel Eliot. *The Oxford History of the American People.* New

York: Oxford University Press, 1965.

Moss, Randolph. "A Sitting President's Amenability to Indictment and Criminal Prosecution," Assistant Attorney General, Office of Legal Counsel, Oct. 16, 2000.

Neale, Thomas. *The Electoral College: How It Works in Contemporary Presidential Elections* (CRS Report 7-5700 RL32611). Washington, DC: Congressional Research Service, 2016, https://fas.org/sgp/crs/misc/RL32611.pdf.

Olsen, Lise, "Judge Kent Resigns Amid Impeachment proceeding." *Houston Chronicle,* June 25, 2009.

Paschenko, Chris, "U.S. House Approves Kent Impeachment." *Houston Chronicle,* June 20, 2009.

Pfiffner, James. "The President's Broad Power to Pardon and Commute." The Heritage Foundation, July 7, 2007.

Rakove, Jack N. *Original Meanings: Politics and Ideas in the Making of the Constitution.* New York: Alfred A. Knopf, 1996.

Rehnquist, William H. *Grand Inquests: The Historic Impeachments of Samuel Chase and President Andrew Johnson,* New York: William Morrow, 1992.

The Royal Collection Trust. https://www.royalcollection.org.uk/collection/31700/st-edwards-crown (accessed May 16, 2017).

The Royal Family. Royal. UK: https://www.royal.uk/search?tags[0]=Treaty%20of%20Dover (accessed May 14, 2017).

Simpson, Alex. *A Treatise on Federal Impeachments.* Philadelphia, Law Association of Philadelphia, 1916.

Sirica, John J. *To Set the Record Straight.* New York: W. W. Norton and Co., 1979.

Stathis, Stephen. *Congressional Resolutions on Presidential Impeachment: A Historical Overview* (CRS Report No. 98-763 GOV). Washington, DC: Congressional Research Service, 1998.

Tennissen, Marilyn. "Fifth Circuit Denies Kent's Disability Status, Recommends Impeachment." *SouthEast Texas Record,* May 28, 2009.

U.S. Congress, *Constitution with Index and Declaration of Independence,* 108th Cong., 1st sess, H. Doc. 108-96, 21st edition.

U.S. Senate Website. https://www.senate.gov/artandhistory/history/common/briefing/Senate_Impeachment_Role.htm.

Whitney, David C. *Founders of Freedom in America: Lives of the Men Who Signed the Constitution.* Chicago: J. G. Ferguson, 1965.

Whitney, David C. *Founders of Freedom in America; Lives of the Men Who Signed the Declaration of Independence.* Chicago: J. G. Ferguson, 1965.

Witherspoon, Tommy. "Rep. Flores: Judge's Punishment Did Not Fit the Crime," *Waco Tribune-Herald,* January 22, 2016.

ACKNOWLEDGMENTS

I give thanks to Seth Davidson, Governor Mark White, Ed Supkis, Grant Harvey, and new friend Dennis Johnson, his artists and his entire staff—particularly my brilliant editor Taylor Sperry; managing editor, Susan Rella; and the equally important and astute copy editor, Lyn Rosen—at Melville House. While any errors in this work are mine, not theirs, each friend and colleague provided a rich mix of inspiration, art, criticism, and support in this journey of learning.

BARBARA A. RADNOFSKY was the first woman in Texas history to run as the Democratic nominee for the U.S. Senate in 2006, and the first to run as the Democratic nominee for Texas attorney general in 2010. A magna cum laude graduate of the University of Houston, where she enrolled at age sixteen, and the University of Texas School of Law, Radnofsky has practiced law for nearly four decades. She lives in Houston.